Making Pots

A ceramicist's guide

Stefan Andersson

Photography by Calle Stoltz

PAVILION

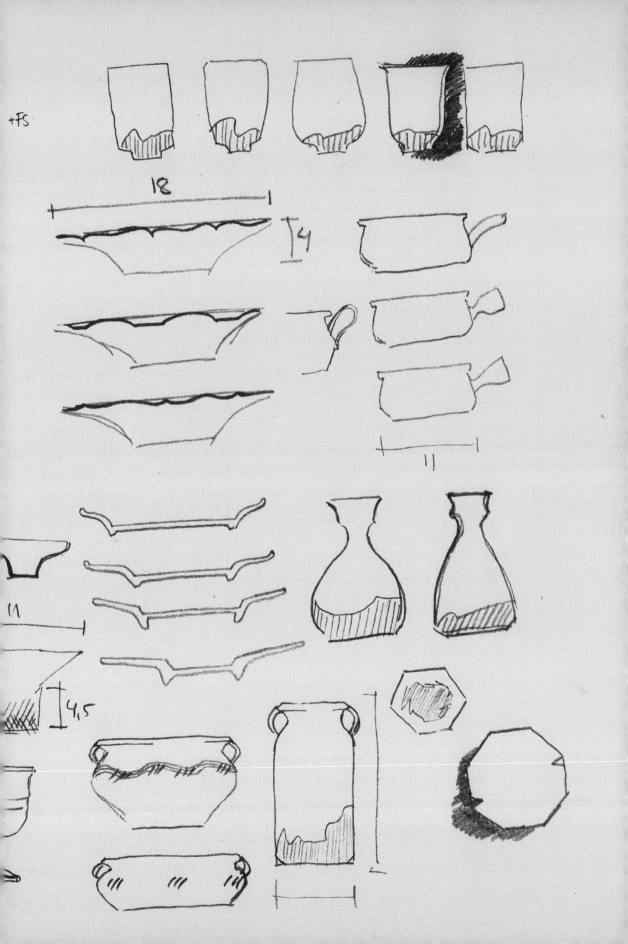

CONTENTS

My pottery is located in the little village of Alvik outside Leksand in Sweden. For almost 20 years, the majority of my days have been all about clay and I've had the opportunity to show my work at galleries, stores and restaurants all over the world. My workshop is in the basement of the house where I live with my family, a good arrangement as it means I can easily look after my pots. One pot might need turning over and another might need covering in plastic to make sure it doesn't dry out too much. On the slope below the house are my kilns and wood stacks and below those is lake Siljan.

I didn't end up here because of a long-standing love for clay. Initially, it was more like an escape from boring university studies, and slowly I realized that the work of a potter suited me. It's a winning combination of hand, head and creativity.

Clay can be many things. For some a laborious livelihood, for others a serious hobby and for some an interest that there's never enough time for. What I like about clay is that it is so pliant, and that it has something to offer everyone.

In this book I will show you how to get started with pottery. Not a lot is required for you to make your first bowl, but at the same time, any of the steps in the process – wedging, forming, glazing and firing – can go wrong and you'll have to start all over again. Frustrating, possibly, but at the same time its greatest charm. A craft to grow with.

Stefan Andersson

BASICS

In earlier times, potters had no choice but to use clay from a nearby field. Designs were determined by how pliable the clay was, any decoration was a result of the forming technique and firing was fine-tuned to prevent cracks, blisters and breakages. With limited means, it was possible to make good pots that easily measure up to today's standards, in terms of both user-friendliness and design.

For those outside the pottery world, porcelain is the only clay there is, but a potter divides clay into three different groups – earthenware, stoneware and porcelain. They are all made from weathered rock, and share many other characteristics. The classifications exist mainly to help us decide to what temperature they should be fired.

Earthenware clay is darker and naturally easy to work with. This is due to it having travelled a long way from its origins, accumulating soil, organic material and other particles along the way.

Porcelain clay on the other hand, is relatively pure resulting in its white colour. It is often regarded as difficult to work with, as it's more delicate and unstable on the wheel, but it's just different to work with (and requires some adjustments to the techniques used).

In between these two groups we find **stoneware clay,** which comes in many different varieties.

An important thing to note about the different characteristics of the three groups is that earthenware is fired to a temperature a couple of hundred degrees lower than stoneware and porcelain. As a rule, earthenware clay is difficult to make waterproof, while porcelain and stoneware are, in principle, completely waterproof after firing.

Plasticity is the clay's ability to stretch and bend. A clay with high plasticity, for example, is good for throwing since it can be stretched without cracking, while a clay with less plasticity is better for rolling and for making larger objects. The appearance of many older pots – from the 19th century and earlier – can tell us about the limitations of the local clay, whether it had low plasticity or impurities, for example.

Today we rarely work with clays taken straight from the ground, and the distinctions between earthenware, porcelain and stoneware are becoming more and more blurred. Instead, clays are produced by mixing many different ingredients together so that suppliers can provide reliable clay again and again. This has also opened up the possibility of making earthenware clays that can be fired to higher temperatures and novelties such as black porcelain.

By adding a substance called **grog** (fired and ground clay), clays can be altered further to develop different characteristics.

The use of grog is likely to have begun with the first broken pot and gives the clay sturdiness and durability. Depending on how coarse the grog is, the clay will become more or less suitable for different forming techniques. Clays come in various grog grades.

Many pottery studios and schools choose not to use both earthenware and stoneware together. The risk is that earthenware is accidentally fired to the higher temperature that is used for stoneware, which can lead to severe damage to the kiln. If you are experimenting with different types of clay, best practice is to fire smaller samples on a shelf that you aren't precious about, or perhaps in a bowl that you don't like so much.

Four clays that I use in my work.
At the top is a stoneware clay that
contains iron and a little bit of
sand. To the left is a reliable white
stoneware clay. To the right, a coarse-
grogged natural stoneware clay.
The grey colour comes from the high
concentration of organic material in
the clay. At the front
is a dense white porcelain clay that
turns transparent in the kiln.

When it comes to throwing pots, most people prefer a grog grade of up to 0.2mm, while those who handbuild large plates or fire raku (see page 52) often prefer a coarser grade. But there are exceptions, and one of my most popular cups is thrown in a clay with 0.5mm grog. This gives a body (see image caption) with a lot of character, but my fingertips need days to recover after throwing, to get their fingerprints back.

Those who are more observant will note that there's a difference between one grog and another. Some grogs are like crushed rocks while others can be smooth like sand. Each will contribute something, adding a specific characteristic during the production process, giving small contrasts in both colour and structure after firing.

In all cultures there are examples of potters adding organic material to clay to improve its quality. A common additive used to be animal manure. A modern version is to mix in paper pulp. Just a small addition of paper makes the clay a lot stronger, which means that large objects can be moved and dried without them cracking. I mix sawdust into my larger pieces to prevent cracking, but fibres such as cotton or reed also work well.

Most distributors sell different types of ready-mixed paper clay. These clays contain a significant amount of paper, giving them some exciting qualities, the main one being that it's possible to add fresh clay to already dried clay without them cracking.

Making your own paper clay is easy, but don't make more than you need, as it gets mouldy quickly.

RECIPE FOR PAPER CLAY

1. Tear 500g (2 cups) newspaper or toilet paper into shreds and add 500ml (2 cups) water to the shreds.

2. Leave to stand for a few hours and then blend the mixture into a smooth paste.

3. Stir in 500g (2 cups) completely dry clay in little crumbs and leave until dissolved.

4. Tip out the paper clay onto a piece of fabric and leave it to dry until it's workable but not sticky.

The paper will burn out in the kiln, resulting in smoke and ash. If there's too much ash in the clay, the pot will melt and collapse. In principle, mixing in a lot of paper or other organic material means that you slowly but surely turn your stoneware clay into an earthenware clay.

There are a number of internationally renowned clays such as Shigaraki clay (named after the Japanese town famed for its pottery), Albany slip (from the US town which originally had a clay hill), and Jingdezhen porcelain (from the town in China). What these clays all have in common is that they, by and large, no longer exist. That clays disappear is a reality for all potters, and it's hard to find a potter who doesn't mourn a favourite clay. But as clay is one of earth's most abundant resources, we're not in any risk of it running out altogether.

I tend to go for slightly darker stoneware clays in my workshop, but all clays have their place, as long as they find the right shape. As a rule, I choose grogged clays, since the slightly coarser surface suits my projects and the extra durability comes in handy when wood-firing. Occasionally I mix in a little sand with the clay as well. I have also mixed in coffee grounds to create a lively body when the coffee burns out in the kiln.

$\longrightarrow$
For the potter, the word 'ware' means objects that are made of clay. A potter making utilitarian ware will be concerned with the thickness of a pot's walls because this is important for the overall feel of the finished pot. The body's texture and firing will affect the appearance of the pot and how it feels in the hand.

Clay preparation

Historically, in their first year an apprentice would have been tasked with cleaning the studio and wedging (kneading) the clay, in the second year, making simple objects and in the third year they would get involved in manufacturing. Even so, it probably won't take you a year to learn to wedge clay.

When you remove clay from its packaging it generally needs to be prepared. This is mainly because the water will have dispersed unevenly in the clay, but also because clay becomes easier to work with if it's brought to life with a bit of wedging. When clay is reused it's also probably that it will need wedging to remove air bubbles. It's often said that pots can break from the presence of air bubbles – this isn't entirely true. But air bubbles can make both throwing and rolling out more difficult if they appear in the wrong place.

If the clay is too soft you can leave it to air-dry before preparing it and if it's too hard you can add water. An easy way to make a slightly too-dry clay soft again is to make a few holes in the clay packet (piercing right through the bag) and lower it into a bucket of water. Leave to stand for 15 minutes and then take out the packet of clay. After that you can wedge the clay into a consistent texture. Even easier is to leave the bag of clay to stand in water for a day so that the added moisture evens itself out.

I prefer to wedge the clay in my workshop with the stack and slam method (see page 24), and I have to confess that over the years I have cut corners more and more. These days, I sometimes feel that it's enough to drop the packet on the floor a few times without wedging the clay at all before I start working. For beginners, however, it's a good idea to wedge the clay as it will make it easier to work with. For the same reason, I always prepare the clay more carefully when I am throwing thinner or larger shapes.

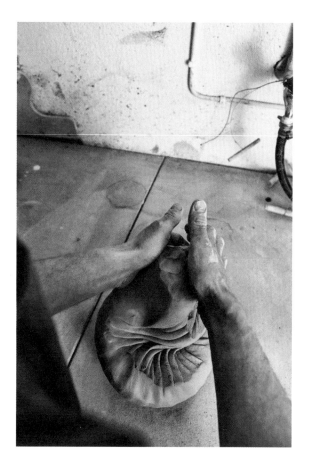

$\longrightarrow$
You can make a simple wire for the stack and slam method from a 2-mm (1/16-in) thick wire, a turnbuckle, wire clip and two firmly attached hooks. Your work surface should be at least 70 x 70cm (27½ x 27½in) and made from a material that will absorb moisture, for example particle board.

SPIRAL WEDGING

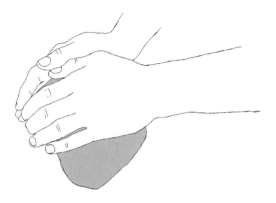

1. Position your hands close to each other. When spiral wedging your clay, only knead the top right corner of the clay. After each action, check and correct your position and start working your way back to the corner if you have slid away from it.

2. To start, press down lightly with your left hand while keeping the lump of clay stable with a cupped right hand.

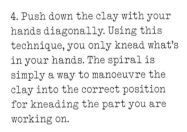

3. Tip up the clay, rotate it slightly anti-clockwise (counterclockwise) and move your grip.

4. Push down the clay with your hands diagonally. Using this technique, you only knead what's in your hands. The spiral is simply a way to manoeuvre the clay into the correct position for kneading the part you are working on.

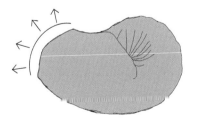

5. Repeat steps 3 and 4 approx. 30 times if you have a small lump of clay and up to 60 times if you have a larger lump (more than 3kg/6lb 8oz).

6. To finish off, move the left hand further and further away from the right hand for every action until the spiral becomes completely worked into the clay.

Clay preparation

TROUBLESHOOTING

- If you get pain in your wrists from wedging, use a softer clay and aim to keep your wrists as straight as possible when pushing down.
- If tho lump doesn't quite come together in a spiral, be more gentle with your left hand.

It's easy to press too hard with your left hand at each turn. A better method is to double the number of actions using half the strength.

- If you get air trapped in the clay, the most common cause is that the lump gets too concave in your cupped hand. Pinch

carefully with your right hand to make sure that the clay is convex in the hand.
- If there's too much distance between each fold of the spiral, your grip for each action is too large. As a rule, many smaller turns are better than fewer larger turns.

These days I only spiral wedge towards the end of the process to get a nicely shaped lump of clay for throwing. I do the majority of my preparation work using the stack and slam method (see next page). These two techniques have their roots in two different craft traditions. The first one, spiral wedging, requires practice and attentiveness to the clay. The second one, the stack and slam technique, is less romantic but more powerful. Each has its own use, but spiral wedging generally takes longer to master. If you are persistent, you will learn – so don't give up!

If you have two different clays, you can mix them together to create a new clay body. If you choose to stack and slam or spiral wedge the clay you will need to use a fair bit of elbow grease before the clays are mixed together. But combining clays without fully mixing them can also be used as a decorative effect. English agateware and Japanese nerikomi ceramics are examples of traditions where different coloured clays are mixed together to either produce a marbled effect, or to create precise patterns.

A good opportunity to mix different clays together is when you are reclaiming dry clay. Completely dry clay quickly dissolves in water and can be mixed into a smooth paste that will turn into a workable clay again once dried to the right consistency. Drying clay can take time. Many people choose to have a plaster bat in the workshop to speed up the process. You can easily make your own plaster bat by screwing together a wooden frame and then pouring plaster into it. You can buy plaster from your clay supplier, and there are usually instructions on the bag specifying the proportions of water and plaster. I don't have room for plaster bats in my workshop. Instead I leave the clay to air dry on a piece of particle board, which means the clay usually takes an extra day to dry.

STACK AND SLAM WEDGING

1. Hold the clay over the wire and slam it straight down towards the surface. The throw needs to be hard enough to cut the clay into two pieces and to make the pieces collapse slightly from the force.

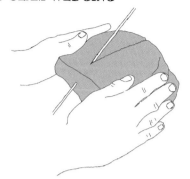

2. Turn the two pieces so that the cut sides are facing away from you.

3. Lift one of the pieces by tipping it up into your hands.

4. Slam that piece down onto the other piece. Both cut sides should still be facing away from you.

5. Turn the lump so that the cut sides face towards you.

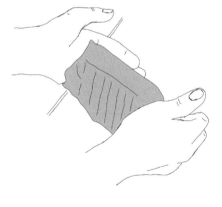

6. Repeat steps 1 to 5 approximately 20 to 30 times.

TROUBLESHOOTING
- If you have worked air into the clay during wedging, you need to make sure that both surfaces you slam together in step 4 are smooth.

- If the clay sticks to the table, it's either too wet or the work surface doesn't absorb enough water. Leave the clay and the table to dry a little and use less force in steps 1 and 4.

- If you can't get enough force into step 1, try to lift the clay higher and throw it on the way down instead of just dropping it. A good slam is similar to the movement you would use with a hammer or an axe.

Drying

During the drying process, clay will shrink, and this can cause problems. Sometimes cracks will appear straight away and once they do, they unfortunately tend to grow. There is a glimmer of hope – the problem can be avoided with practice.

When clay has dried slightly, we say it has become **leather hard**. In this state, the clay will keep its shape, but it's still possible to press a fingernail into the surface. If the clay is left to dry a little longer, the last of its flexibility will disappear and the clay will become significantly lighter in colour. This state is called **bone dry** and we can now only scrape or crack the clay. Just after the bone dry state, the clay can be fired so it becomes ceramic material. It's easy to forget that clay can also be used in an unfired state, for example in the magnificent adobe mosques in Mali and for the walls in timber-framed houses here in Sweden.

One problem that can occur during drying is that the different parts of the ware dry at different speeds, which can lead to cracks. In order to prevent this, try to make the walls of your ware an even thickness and build them in the same way. If you looked at a cross-section of a bowl, it would have evenly thick walls throughout. You should take extra care to shape the base, which can easily be forgotten while you work on the walls. With experience you can incorporate further dimensions into your work and often a design will demand you break these simple rules. For example, it can be advantageous to make the base slightly thinner, and then there might be a need to make the lower part of the wall a bit thicker so that the bowl keeps its shape during the firing.

During drying the clay will lose much of its water content and will shrink by approximately 6 per cent. It will also lose about 30 per cent of its weight. It's often possible to feel when a pot is dry enough to be fired from its weight. Otherwise, an old trick is to place the pot against your cheek – if it feels colder than the surroundings it is still too wet to be fired.

During the making process try not to let some parts of the ware become significantly wetter than others. Leaving water to stand in the base of a pot, or adding too much water during throwing for example, can easily lead to cracks during the drying process. In some cases however, it will actually help to wet the clay a little more, such as when you are attaching a handle to a cup that you've thrown the day before. Placing a drop of water where you want to attach the handle creates a bridge between the two different dry surfaces and lowers the risk of cracks.

Beyond the making process, there are further things you can do to avoid problems. The first is to choose a clay that has less shrinkage. It could, for example, be a clay containing more grog or paper. But even two clays containing the same amount of grog can have very different qualities. In other words, it can be worth trying a different clay if you encounter problems in the drying process.

The other way to avoid cracks is to control the drying process. Most things that crack will do so at the point when the clay changes colour (that is when it goes from leather hard to bone dry). The reason is that the more dry, inflexible clay wants to shrink but cannot and this leads to cracks.

Imagine a bowl that is left to dry completely in the open: it will become bone dry from the top down, from the rim to the foot. When bowls are allowed to dry in this way, problems will usually emerge towards the end of the drying process when it's the turn of the base to dry and shrink. Since the walls are already dry and hard, the bowl's diameter has been fixed and the base will crack as it shrinks.

28

The crack usually takes the form of an 's' shape and is therefore called an s-crack. The most common way to avoid s-cracks is to turn the ware upside down during drying. This way the base will dry, and the rim of the bowl will stay moist for longer. Some shapes can be difficult to turn upside down however, for example if they have an uneven rim, such as a jug with a spout. In these cases, you can achieve the same result by covering the ware with plastic during drying.

In other words, the key to success is to make sure that pots dry evenly. Draughts or sunlight can also cause problems. In my workshop I get issues as soon as the humidity drops in winter, and there's a greater need to slow down the drying process with help from plastic or by covering the wares with an old sheet (see page 33). Interestingly, pots can actually be dried very fast, as long as the speed of drying is evenly distributed throughout the shape. In practice, that often means that the speed of drying is slowed down. As a rule, smaller bowls and cups need four to five days to dry enough so that they're ready to be fired;

$\leftarrow$

It can be tempting to mend cracks that appear during the drying process, but as a general rule, it is better to start again and reuse the clay instead. This way you will become more skilled at making rather than mending. If you still want to try and mend, my advice is to thoroughly rework the affected area: use a tool to push the clay into the crack, as more superficial mending will rarely be enough.

a plate can need another day or two. Exact drying times vary from workshop to workshop.

Sometimes it is necessary to completely halt the drying process of a small piece of pottery. Covering with plastic is usually a good solution, but if you find yourself in this situation often, I suggest that you make a small damp box. A damp box (see below) generates high humidity around the clay and the clay will not get dryer than the surrounding air.

When you start working with larger clay objects there are additional things to keep in mind during drying. A large slab will often shrink several centimetres and can easily crack in the middle if it is unable to pull one edge towards the other in the drying process. You can ease the resistance by placing a few sheets of newspaper or fabric underneath. When it comes to slabbed and handbuilt objects, I prefer to leave the ware to dry tilted, so that gravity helps pull it together as it shrinks. Thrown wares don't need the same help due to the clay being worked differently.

You will often notice a small change in the shape of a piece during the drying process. For example, the rim on a plate can start curling inwards, only to go back into the shape of its original form. The reason for this is that the rim dries more quickly and will retract slightly before the rest of the shape catches up. On some objects the shape will never go back to its original form. Large cylinders often bend inwards a little after drying, when the top edges have pulled together more. Crafty potters can use this technique to their advantage and make curved plates by leaving flat plate-sized slabs to curl upwards in the drying process.

MAKE YOUR OWN DAMP BOX
• Take a plastic storage box with a lid of a suitable size and cast approximately 5cm (2in) of plaster in the bottom of the box. Follow the instructions on the packet for mixing Gypsum plaster. When the plaster has cured (set), keep it damp by continually adding a little water.
• A good alternative to plaster is to press out a layer of moist clay into the plastic box instead.

Keep it damp with help from a spray bottle of water. Place a layer of fabric in the box as well so that the clay doesn't stick to your pieces.

Glazing

The terms 'glaze' and 'glass' are closely related and in most cases it's just a glassy surface we're aiming to achieve when glazing. Anyone who wholeheartedly throws themselves into the world of glazing will eventually pick up a lot of chemistry knowledge, but you can go a long way with trial and error – just like potters have done for millennia.

The first stoneware glazes

Around 2000 years ago potters discovered how to fire kilns to higher temperatures, which opened the door to using high-firing bodies: stoneware and porcelain. The kilns were wood-fired, and potters suddenly noticed how the ash from the wood started to melt and turn into a glaze on the wares. It's likely that many potters helped the natural glazing get going by sprinkling extra ash on top of the pots, developing the first ash glazes in the form of ash and water. These glazes had their flaws but by adding a small amount of clay to the glaze, it became a lot more reliable – both in the glazing and the firing process. Different ashes and clays could produce a muted colour spectrum from yellow to green and sometimes even red and purple.

To make your own ash glaze, you can collect ash from your fireplace or wood-fired stove. The result will vary depending on which type of wood you have burnt, and true enthusiasts look for ash from different types of wood. Personally, I take ash from the wood-fired kiln and go along with whatever glaze I end up with.

Before you use the ash, you should sift it using a standard mesh sieve to remove any lumps, nails and other bits. Since ash is slightly caustic, you want to avoid getting it into your lungs, so do this outside wearing a protective mask. If you cover the sieve with a wet towel and shake the ash straight into a bucket this will also help you to avoid the dust. Mix water with the ash and you have got a simple ash glaze. The water in an ash glaze will feel soapy and will also become slightly caustic, so when you are glazing it's best to wear rubber gloves.

STEFAN'S EASY ASH GLAZE
In glaze recipes, the weight measurements always refer to the dry ingredients. In this recipe the proportions are specified in parts, so if you have 1kg (2lb 3oz) ash you will need to mix 1kg (2lb 3oz) dry clay into the ash. The amount of water isn't specified in glaze recipes so you will have to experiment to see what works. As a rule, ash glazes need to be applied generously, since a lot of the ash will simply burn off in the kiln. Always make a small glaze test for new batches so that you don't damage the kiln.

1 part ash
1 part earthenware clay

Fire to 1200–1300°C (2200–2370°F) for a matt to gloss glaze in a range of colours.

The next step in glaze development came when potters found rocks and sediment that they could grind to make purer glazes. They tested various ingredients from their surroundings and developed localized glazes that then spread further. These simple glazes were mainly developed in China 1000 years ago. Often when we talk about them, they are referred to as the classic Chinese glazes. Perhaps the most common is celadon – a pale transparent glaze – and tenmoku, a black glaze. Many of my recipes build on the explorations of the Chinese. One of the substances they found was whiting. By mixing whiting into the clay used for pots, they could get a really good glaze for utilitarian ware. From a production point of view, it was probably also a relief after working with caustic ash glazes without rubber gloves.

Gives transparency to matt glazes, depending on the composition of the clay and the firing. White clays will generally give a pale yellow to a light green glaze, but you can also use darker clays and see what happens. I usually make this glaze from Witgert's white clay number 11 and use it for raw glazing. I rarely get a good end result if the glaze is too thin. (See page 41 on slips and raw glazing for the method).

2 parts white stoneware clay
  without grog
1 part whiting

Fire to 1260—1300°C (2300—2370°F), the hotter the glossier.

Glaze thickness and firing temperature

There is no 'right glaze thickness'. The same glaze can have a different appearance depending on its thickness. What we can say is that glazes rarely exhibit a special or unique character if they are applied thinly, but then, this could create the particular appearance that you're after. It's down to personal taste, so I suggest that you try a few different glaze tests.

I usually prefer to mix glaze with water until it has the thickness of single cream, or slightly thinner, otherwise it's difficult to get a good covering of glaze when raw glazing. Many glazes that I use also contain ash, which will largely burn off early on in the firing without turning into glaze. Transparent glazes, such as those bought ready made, generally don't have to be any thicker than milk to give a nice transparent coat over the clay. A word of warning: a thicker layer of glaze increases the risk of the glaze dripping off the pot.

When glazing bisque-fired wares (see page 47) the thickness of the glaze is less important, as you can easily get a thicker glaze by dipping the pot into the glaze for a longer time.

The same can be said for firing temperature. Every glaze will appear different at different temperatures. Often there's a cone (see page 126) or temperature

specified on store-bought glazes (and also in my recipes in this book), which can be used as a good starting point.

If you fire to a higher temperature, the glaze will shift more and become shinier, and vice versa if you go down in temperature. Some glazes can completely change colour and character by just altering the thickness and firing temperature, so go ahead and experiment and learn to know your glazes. The same batch of glaze can give you several different appearances.

Glazing ingredients

Something that can seem overwhelming when it comes to glazes is the large number of different ingredients available. For my own practice I choose to use only a handful. The modern potter also has the opportunity to buy high-quality ready-made glazes.

One important ingredient is feldspar. Feldspar is easy to use, since it makes a fairly balanced glaze on its own. The most common types of feldspar are **potash feldspar** and **nepheline syenite**. They have slightly different characteristics. Generally we can say that nepheline syenite melts at a lower temperature but has a tendency to cause slightly more crazing (see page 49) in the glazing surface. Potters have used feldspar for thousands of years and today most glazes still use feldspar as a base.

JAN-ÅKE'S SHINO

Makes a white to orange-red glaze. Shino is a classic glaze from Japan that comes in many different varieties and is used all over the world. The beauty of traditional Japanese shino lies in its 'defects' — it doesn't melt fully and crawls into beads when applied. Glaze thickly and unevenly and see what happens.

3 parts nepheline syenite
1 part ball clay (see page 38)

Fire to 1260—1300°C (2300—2370°F), for varying results.

In Jan-Åke's shino we come across **ball clay**, which – along with **china clay** (**kaolin**) – is the most common clay used in glazes. They aren't very good clays for pot making, but are excellent for glazes. China clay and ball clay are relatively similar, the choice between them mainly affects how the glazes bond with the pots.

Together, whiting, potash feldspar, nepheline syenite, ball clay and china clay give you a broad base for exploring glazes, but I mustn't forget to mention **silica**. It is also known as quartz and can be found in clay, wood ash and feldspar – sources that potters have used for a long time. In most glazes, silica is what makes them shiny, but silica itself melts at much higher temperatures than stoneware reaches to use it we have to lower its melting temperature. This is done by adding a substance called a flux. The most common flux for stoneware is whiting, and in traditional earthenware pottery lead was used.

NUKA GLAZE
This is a white, opaque glaze if applied thickly, but transparent and shiny if applied thinly. The ash should be washed to prevent the glaze turning yellow-brown in colour.

To wash ash, fill a bucket halfway with sieved ash. Top the bucket up with water and stir. Leave to stand for a day and then carefully discard the water that is sitting on top of the ash. Top up with fresh water, stir, leave to stand and discard in the same way at least five times. The aim is to flush out the water-soluble substances from the ash. You will notice that the water becomes less and less soapy each time.

1 part washed ash
1 part feldspar
1 part silica

Fired to 1260–1300°C
(2300–2370°F).

Once you have found a glaze that you like, whether it's homemade or store-bought, you can continue to develop it by adding other substances. To add colour, use different metallic oxides and stains. Stains work fairly intuitively and increasing the amount will give you more of the colour than it says on the bag. Note that all stains have a maximum temperature, after which they will start to lose colour.

Metallic oxides can be a bit trickier to predict and it will be necessary to carry out glazing tests using increasing amounts of the oxide to see what happens when firing. Stains contain the same metallic oxides that we work with in their pure state, but they have been processed commercially to make them more reliable as a colourant.

SUGGESTIONS FOR ADDING
COLOURING TO GLAZES IN
AN ELECTRIC KILN
• Yellow: Add 1–5% iron oxide
• Orange: Add 5–10% rutile
  (contains titanium dioxide)
• Blue: Add 0.25–2% cobalt oxide
• Green: Add 1–5% copper oxide
• Red: Add 1–20% red stain
• Dark red effect: 10% iron oxide
  and 10% bone ash
• Black: 6% iron oxide, 3%
  manganese oxide and 1%
  cobalt oxide

In addition to these ingredients, there is a range of other substances that can alter the base glaze in different ways. Some will alter the colouring so that they turn a completely different colour in the kiln. Some will make glazes matt, or more scratch-proof, while others are used to compensate for shortcomings in the base glaze. Two common ingredients are tin oxide and zirconium silicate, which are used for turning transparent glazes opaque. Tin glaze came to Europe with the Moors in the 10th century and forms the basis for rich faience pottery.

Mixing glazes

It's easy to mix glazes and when you want to test recipes at home you can buy new ingredients from your supplier. Read up a little to find out the qualities that different ingredients produce and also how to use glazes safely. There are many good books on glazes and your supplier has a responsibility to inform you of any risks that might come with certain ingredients. Most substances don't carry any specific hazards – just make sure you minimize dust when using the substances and wear a mask.

For mixing glazes you will need scales, a bucket with a lid, a smaller container, a scoop or a spoon, an old stick blender and the ingredients. I use old-fashioned balance scales to weigh ingredients that are 100g (3½ oz) and heavier. If I'm dealing with lighter weights, I use letter scales for better precision.

> Keep your work surface dust free and use a mask if it gets dusty. The mask should have a particle filter to protect against toxic dust, which a regular face mask doesn't.

1. Calculate how much of each ingredient you will need. A total weight of 50g (1¾ oz) will be enough for a few samples, while 4–6kg (9–13lb) will fill a standard 10-litre (2-gallon) bucket. For recipes using ratios, it is fairly straightforward to imagine each part as a certain weight, but if the recipe is written down as percentages you may have to use a calculator.

2. Place the container on the scales and set the scales to zero so that you don't have to take the weight of the container into account.

3. Label the bucket and lid with the name of your glaze and add a little water to the bottom of the bucket.

4. Weigh out each ingredient separately and carefully add them to the bucket. Double check the weights and the substances, it is usually at this stage that errors occur.

5. Add water and blend to a thick creamy consistency. Some substances will expand in water and some won't so let the mixture rest for 10 minutes. Dilute the glaze further with a little bit of water until you've got the right consistency (note that cheaper stick blenders can break if you work them too hard, so leave it to rest if it starts to feel hot). I used to use sieves with different-sized meshes and sieve the glaze until smooth, but nowadays I think this method is more convenient.

6. The glaze is now ready to be used. Fire a glaze test before glazing and firing large amounts.

TROUBLESHOOTING

- If the glaze is too thick, add more water. When you glaze, the pot will absorb slightly more water than minerals, so you might have to add a bit more water to the glaze occasionally.
- If the glaze is too thin, you will have to get rid of excess water. The easiest way to do this is to leave the glaze to stand for a couple of days to allow the minerals to sink and then carefully discard the water that has separated at the top.
- If the minerals have sunk to the bottom of the bucket, it's because the recipe contains little or no clay. A trick is to add 5 per cent bentonite to the glaze. Bentonite is a fine-grain clay that will only marginally affect the appearance of a glaze, while mitigating the problem. Bentonite cannot be mixed straight into water. You will either have to mix it in with the dry ingredients when making the glaze, or alternatively, mix the bentonite thoroughly with a small amount of glaze that you then add back to the batch.
- If the glaze suddenly starts to behave differently, it can mean it has separated. Try to stir the glaze thoroughly, since it might be that some of the ingredients have sunk to the bottom of the bucket and set.

Slips and raw glazing

Slip is clay mixed with water that you can pour, dip or brush onto your pots. Usually this is done when the pot is leather hard, but there are slips that are also used for bisque-fired wares. In many pottery traditions, this was the only way to make white pots, as white clay was rare and difficult to work with.

In Korea, for example, buncheong ceramics were developed alongside porcelain as an alternative for the masses. In addition to being rare, the white clay didn't bond well with stoneware clay, so the Koreans developed their own aesthetic by brushing white slip onto dark clay. The same story has been repeated in many parts of the world and Korea's Buncheong ceramics can be said to be related to Swedish earthenware, Japanese hakeme and English slipware. All possess their own interesting characteristics, the common factor being white slip over dark clay.

MAKE YOUR OWN SLIP
Choose a clay without grog for your slip. Slice the clay into thin discs, approx. 5mm (1/4in), and leave to dry. Once they are thoroughly dry (bone dry), drop them into a bucket of water. Resist the temptation to stir and leave the discs to disintegrate in the water. Once all the clay has disintegrated, blend it smooth using an old stick blender or run it twice through a sieve with mesh size 100. You will always need to do a test to see how the slip sticks to your clay.

A raw glaze is a glaze that you apply to the pot before firing. This way you don't have to fire the pot several times (see the section on firing on page 46). For raw glazing, you can use the exact same methods and troubleshooting tips as for slips.

However, since a raw-glazed pot hasn't finished shrinking, there are a few requirements when it comes to the glaze. As a rule, the recipe will need to contain at least one-third clay. If you glaze thinly, most glazes will work however, so go ahead and try it out. Most recipes in this book are fine for raw

glazing, but it will to a certain extent depend on what clay the pot is made out of.

BLUE CLAY GLAZE
This glaze gives a dark brown to black glaze depending on the clay. If it cools quickly it will become glossy, but when cooled slowly, matt yellow to green dots will appear in the glaze. You can also try different earthenware clays without grog for a large spectrum of colours of raw glazes.

1 part grey earthenware clay

Fire to 1260–1300°C (2300–2370°F).

Applying slip is largely dependent on timing. I wait until the pot is as dry as it can be without it starting to change colour – leather hard but not bone dry. At this stage, the pot can absorb a little bit of water without becoming unstable. If a pot has dried unevenly, I cover it in plastic and leave it to stand for a day. I also adjust the design to make sure I've got a grip-friendly base or other designated place where a fingerprint can be left after applying the slip. Before applying, I make sure that the slip has the right consistency. If it's too thin, it won't give enough of a coating and if it's too thick, the pot can crack, or the slip can flake at the rim or on the exterior of the pot. I test the thickness by dipping in a finger to make sure it easily drips off, but still covers it enough so that the skin colour can't be seen through it.

Applying slip to different shapes
I hold plates at the foot ring, and if necessary, let them rest lightly against my forearm. While holding the plate over a large bucket, I pour slip over half of the plate. I rotate the plate and repeat with the other side, after which I shake off excess slip with three or four firm shakes. Sometimes I need to use both hands in addition to holding a finger on the rim so that I do not lose my grip when shaking it. I finish off by running a finger along the bottom to catch any drips that have formed. I rarely apply slip to the bottom of plates.

I coat bowls by filling them just over halfway with slip, then, carefully swirl the slip around the edge before pouring it out. I shake off any excess slip and use a damp sponge to remove any dribbles. Not filling the whole bowl with slip means that I can put some force behind pouring the slip out and that way avoid unnecessary mess.

I grip vases across the foot ring. I fill them two-thirds with slip and pour it out again while rotating the pot. If I manage to get the slip to drip out of the pot along the whole rim as I turn it, the inside usually gets completely coated. Immediately afterwards, I dip the pot into the slip and shake it off with three or four firm shakes. I rarely coat smaller vases on the inside with slip, but I like to use a glaze inside for this to make the vase more waterproof and easier to clean.

> In many ways using slip is best suited to larger production runs, when individual pots are less important. Under these circumstances you can work quickly and with a flow, which works well for many of the traditional techniques that are associated with slip decorating. Slip will weaken the pot, so it's good to handle the pot for as little time as possible, taking great care as you work.

Sometimes I apply slip roughly with a brush as a kind of primitive decoration. Often I'm looking for simple patterns or to create a contrast to the sense of symmetry that comes with thrown objects. For this I prefer a hard, preferably worn, brush and thicker slip. It's possible to achieve an even surface by applying slip with a brush, but I recommend using a soft brush, thinner slip and brushing over the object several times using varying brush strokes.

Everyone who uses slips and raw glazes will experience pots collapsing or cracking. What causes these problems is that we are adding moisture back into the clay so that it then quickly reverts back to leather hard or wetter. I have identified two reasons for failure. The first is collapse due to the clay becoming over-saturated with water, causing it to lose its stability. The other is cracks appearing due to tensions between areas that are coated with slip and areas that are uncoated, or due to the pot having areas of uneven dryness to start off with.

TROUBLESHOOTING
- If the pot collapses you can try leaving it for a little longer before applying slip next time, or try coating the inside first, leave it for a day and then coat the outside.
- If the slip is too thin, it's best to get rid of some water. It's rarely feasible to dip the pot into the slip for a longer time, since it will then easily become over-saturated, causing it to collapse. One alternative however is to leave the first coat to dry for a day and then apply a new coat. This technique can also be used to apply slip followed by raw glaze.
- If the slip is peeling off the edge of the pot as it dries, it's because there is a discrepancy between the shrinkage of the clay and the slip. Apply a thinner coat of the slip or run a finger along the rim to remove the slip along the edge. If you look at old pots, you'll see that this is a common solution that has become an aesthetic in its own right.
- If the slip ends up forming puddles in the pot you might need to thin the slip out with a little water so that it's easier to shake off any excess. If the coat of slip is very uneven, it's easy for cracks to appear at these points.
- If handles fall off when applying the slip, it is usually due to weak attachment to the

pot. Wider areas of contact or a more secure join should solve the problem.

- If a handle breaks off and a part of the pot also comes away with it, it is usually due to a discrepancy between the thickness of the pot and the handle. Give the next piece a thicker wall and make sure

that both handle and body are equally dry when applying slip.

- If bowls and plates distort when you apply slip, the problem probably stems from when they were made. Clay demonstrates its 'memory' and will bend in a way that it has been bent at a previous stage. Clays have different degrees of memory and

some clays easier to work with than others.

- If the pot is too dry to apply slip, you can rehydrate it by spraying it with water from a spray bottle and wrapping it in plastic. Repeat the process until the pot is leather hard again.

45

Firing

When clay is fired beyond 600°C (1110°F) it turns into ceramic material and is no longer water soluble. With an increase in temperature the clay becomes harder and eventually waterproof – we say that the clay has sintered.

Most potters will fire a pot twice – first it is bisque fired and then glaze fired. The aim of the bisque firing is to turn the clay into ceramics to make it easier to glaze. After the bisque firing, the wares are taken out of the kiln, glazed and glaze fired in a second firing.

To ensure the pots don't get damaged in the bisque firing we need to follow a schedule. First, the water that is part of the clay needs to be slowly driven off (from 20°C to 650°C/70°F to 1200°F). If this is done too quickly, there is a risk that the pots will explode, which, as a rule, would usually happen at just over 200°C (390°F). Then we reach a critical point at 575°C (1070°F) when large temperature differences in the pot can cause it to crack. Both of these problems are easy to avoid by reducing the speed and allowing the temperature to rise slowly. When you do this, the water has time to evaporate and the temperature can even out.

In my workshop, a standard bisque firing will take 6 hours from room temperature to 600°C (1110°F), followed by a full speed increase up to 980°C (1800°F). With larger pots (larger than 50cm/20in) and thicker wares (thicker than 3cm/1¼in) I follow the slow bisque-firing schedule. For really large pieces and kilns the firing times will become longer and longer. In my large wood-fired kiln (see page 140) I let it take almost 20 hours for the temperature to reach 600°C (1110°F), to make sure that nothing breaks.

There are a lot of substances in the clay that will burn off during bisque firing, and that will come out in the form of unpleasant fumes. In old kiln rooms you can see where the windowpanes have become clouded from gas, and this makes it clear that we should be careful not to expose ourselves to these fumes.

> Electric kilns have ventilation holes in several places for letting out steam and gas and it's good to leave these open up to 650°C (1200°F). After 650°C (1200°F), moisture has been driven out and gases have escaped so you can close the vents to make it easier for the kiln to reach top temperature. That way you will both save energy and protect the kiln from any damaging steam.

After glazing it's time for firing the glaze. Since pots become wet during glazing, you will generally have to raise the kiln temperature slowly at the start of the glaze firing as well. A standard glaze firing in my workshop will take 3 hours up to 300°C (570°F), followed by full speed up to 1280°C (2340°F). Once there, I keep it at a steady temperature for 10 minutes – this is known as soaking.

Soaking makes sure that the temperature in the kiln becomes more even, which allows the glaze to melt evenly throughout the kiln. The top temperature you should fire to depends on the clay and the glaze. If you buy from a wholesaler, materials usually come with recommendations that are a good starting point. It's a good idea to use glazes and clays that fire to the same temperature, but it can be interesting to explore the same glaze at different temperatures if you enjoy experimenting.

After the glaze firing it's advisable to control the cooling. In the same way as 575°C (1070°F) was a sensitive point on the way up, 225°C (440°F) will become a sensitive point on the way down towards cooler temperatures. Thickly glazed objects and

STANDARD BISQUE FIRING
100°C (210°F) per hour ⟶ 600°C (1110°F)
Full speed ⟶ 980°C (1800°F)

SLOW BISQUE FIRING
50°C (120°F) per hour ⟶ 600°C (1110°F)
Full speed ⟶ 980°C (1800°F)

47

some clays are extra sensitive, and to be safe you shouldn't open the kiln before 100°C (210°F). Having said that, some kilns will take an eternity to cool down during the last 300°C (570°F). By opening the vents in an electric kiln you can speed up the process a little. Being a potter takes a lot of patience, but on the flip side, 'Christmas' (kiln opening) comes around more often than for others!

> Many glazes will change characteristics during cooling in the kiln. Many matt glazes are, for example, highly glossy at high temperatures. The matt effect is created by lots of tiny crystals forming on the surface during cooling. By using crystal glazes and specially adapted firing schedules, you can create crystals that are several centimetres in diameter. All kilns have their own natural cooling curves and will therefore give a personal touch to your glazes.

Kiln furniture – kiln shelves and props (see image on page 142–143) – is used when loading the kiln. To prevent wobbling, place each kiln shelf onto three props. The props for each new layer should be placed directly above the props in the previous layer. If you feel that the shelf you just placed is unsteady, you can usually turn one of the props underneath the shelf to lock it into place. There are no storms in the kiln during the firing, so if the ware and the kiln furniture are standing when you close the kiln, they will remain standing after firing.

For bisque firing, it's a good idea to stack things on top of each other to fit as much into the kiln as possible, but when glaze firing, the wares can't touch each other as they would fuse together permanently where you have applied glaze. Some glaze materials will also contaminate each other. A prime example is white tin glazes turning pink in the vicinity of chrome that can be present in green and black glazes.

Since clay can stick to kiln furniture, brush the kiln shelves with a thin layer of kiln wash. It will protect the base of the pots, and if glazes run off the work in the kiln, the shelves will be easier to clean.

You can scrape off any flakes and glaze spillage on the kiln shelf with a trowel or similar tool. If that doesn't work, you can use an angle grinder with a diamond blade. The kiln shelves are delicate and can crack, so it's better to grind and scrape them rather than knock them with a hammer or chisel.

> RECIPE FOR KILN WASH
> Take a standard 10-litre (2-gallon) bucket and pour in 3 litres (6¼pints) water. Weigh and add 2kg (4lb 6½oz) aluminium oxide and 1kg (2lb 3oz) china clay (kaolin). Stir and add more water until you've got a milky mixture. Brush the wash thinly over your kiln shelves. Since you want to avoid getting dust or flakes from the kiln wash in your pots, apply kiln wash only on the top side.

Firing pots twice is a relatively new phenomenon in the history of pottery. In my own practice I usually only fire once. This is possible because I glaze the pots before they're bisque fired and then fire them according to a schedule that is a combination of bisque and glaze firing. This firing is usually called single firing and my schedule looks like this: 6 hours up to 600°C (1110°F), followed by full speed up to 1280°C (2340°F), where I leave it to soak for 10 minutes. I save a lot of time when single firing, because I avoid one of the firings. But it is more demanding, both when it comes to knowledge and timing. (Read more about slips and raw glazing on page 41.)

GLAZE FIRING
100°C (210°F) per hour ⟶ 300°C (570°F)
Full speed ⟶ 1280°C (2340°F)
10 minutes soaking at 1280°C (2340°F)

SINGLE FIRING
100°C (210°F) per hour ⟶ 600°C (1110°F)
Full speed ⟶ 1280°C (2340°F)
10 minutes soaking at 1280°C (2340°F)

TROUBLESHOOTING

- If the glaze crawls, which means it forms beads exposing naked clay in the gaps, you have a glaze with a high surface tension once melted. The surface tension will decrease if you apply a thinner layer. If you have left the wares to stand for a long time before glazing, dust can increase the risk of crawling: remove this by blowing or wiping the pot with a moist sponge before glazing. The clay can also cause problems if it's grogged. Be careful to smooth the clay at the edges and avoid exposing the grog grains with excessive sponge cleaning. Chamois leather is better for achieving smooth edges.
- If the glaze doesn't melt evenly across wares throughout the kiln then extend the soaking time. For small electric kilns you shouldn't soak for more than 30 minutes. If you find that your kiln is firing slightly unevenly in temperature (hot in some parts, cooler in others), turn this into a positive by using a glaze that melts more easily in the cooler parts of the kiln.
- If the glaze doesn't melt as much as it should, it's because the kiln hasn't reached the required temperature. Check that there haven't been any interruptions in the firing. If there haven't, I would suggest that you increase the top temperature of the firing schedule by 10°C (50°F). By using cones (small standardized tests), you can test the temperature of the kiln and adjust the firing schedule accordingly.
- If the glaze crazes more than before, you can try applying a thinner layer of glaze or change the clay. Crazing appears due to differences in shrinkage between glaze and clay, and all clay and glaze combinations will have their own characteristics.
- Blisters appearing on your pots during glaze firing are probably caused either by the clay being fired at too high a temperature or because there are gases in the clay that haven't burnt off. In the first case you just have to lower the firing temperature. In the second case you should try doing a longer soaking during the bisque firing to properly burn off the gases.

Firing might be my most important process for creative expression. Wood firing and salt firing, smoke and ash. Hour-long soaking times versus extremely fast cooling periods in an electric kiln. All to create variation. With this approach you can go far with just a couple of clays and a few glazes.

Kilns: electric, wood-fired and gas

My workshop expands every year. Not so much in square metres, but in the possibilities available. Saying that, I'm always mindful to work with what I've got, rather than dream about the perfect pots I will make in the future. Making good pots is by no means dependent on a spacious, light workshop, the perfect wedging table or a large wood-fired kiln.

The simplest kiln is a hole in the ground where you layer wood, sticks and pots and then set it alight. It's a primitive technique, but it requires more in-depth knowledge to control this kind of kiln than an electric kiln. One firing technique doesn't exclude the other – they can sit side by side in a small pottery.

I fire most of my wares in a large wood-fired kiln below my house and my workshop (see page 140). It is a laborious process that involves a whole load of (pleasant) extra tasks. Watching over the kiln late at night, for example, is something that I enjoy, even if I sometimes wonder what I'm doing. It's not for romantic reasons that I use a wood-fired kiln, but practical ones. A large wood-fired kiln requires time, but it's relatively cheap as it's possible to build it yourself. Besides, it has almost no servicing costs (such as changing the elements in an electric kiln). Personally I appreciate how wood-firing creates variation in even the simplest glazes and clays, so I can focus on design instead of mixing glazes.

Wood-fired kilns come in many different designs and the type I use can be traced back in time a couple of thousand years. The type of kiln is usually called anagama, which is the Japanese name.

←

Plate with cobalt and gold decoration. Gold decals and other enamel colours are fired to a low temperature (700–1000°C/1300–1800°F) after the ware has already been glaze fired.

The choice of name is perhaps a little unfair, since the majority of potters in Asia were using this type of kiln long before the Japanese. The kiln is made up of a chamber with a chimney at one end and a firebox at the other. The space in between was traditionally loaded with pots, bowls and plates, stacked in and on top of each other, since they didn't have access to today's excellent kiln furniture. Typical for this kind of wood-fired kiln is that it will leave a lot of traces from the intense firing in the form of natural variations in colour and surface appearance. Modern wood-fired kilns will burn more efficiently and have a more even temperature, but will also leave less of a trace from firing on the pots.

To build a small wood-fired kiln isn't particularly difficult. In the chapter on building a *pytteugn* there is a step-by-step plan on pages 124–125 for those who want to get going. Follow the plan, but remember that it will take a few rounds of firing before you get the technique right.

In addition to a couple of wood-fired kilns, I have two smaller electric kilns. I use them when I want to achieve a cleaner feeling, when working with white porcelain for example.

Since the glazes I use in the wood-fired kiln will turn out completely differently in the electric kiln, it also gives me the potential to achieve more variation from the same batch of glaze.

My smallest electric kiln only takes 16 litres (around ½ cubic foot) and is super fun to work with. The kiln can be plugged into a standard wall socket and is also easy to move around. It was the first kiln I owned and a great one to start with, since I had a lot of experiments going.

An electric kiln is basically a large toaster. It's heated with an element (a twisted Kanthal wire) that glows when electricity flows through it. To regulate the speed the electricity is controlled by a unit that, with help from a thermocouple, knows what temperature the kiln is at. The elements in the kiln wear slightly with every use. It is possible to increase the lifespan of the elements and save energy by firing to lower temperatures and by using glazes that melt easily. Cleaning the kiln with a vacuum cleaner if you've had any accidents is also a good way to increase the lifespan of the elements.

When the elements are worn out, the kiln will eventually be unable to reach the required temperature. Often it starts with the kiln getting slower in getting up to temperature for each firing.

In electric kilns, glazes and clay have free access to oxygen during the firing, which will have a substantial effect on the look and feel of the wares. Iron oxide, which is found in almost all clays and glazes, will for example turn yellow in a standard electric kiln, but in a kiln with low oxygen, it will turn black, red, green, blue and many other colours.

A firing where oxygen is abundant is called an oxidation firing, while a firing with low oxygen is called a reduction firing. Nowadays, the most common kilns are oxidation kilns, electric kilns in other words. Those who want to practise reduction firing will need a gas, wood-fired or hybrid kiln (an electric kiln with a small gas torch). Traditionally potters also fired with coal and oil, and personally I have even owned a couple of kilns that were fired using deep-frying oil.

Sometimes there's an air of nostalgia around reduction kilns, as if they were superior. But a fun thought experiment is to look back at the time before the electric kiln – we struggled to achieve proper oxidation and smoke, wood and fire mostly created extra work. Electric kilns are without a doubt the most convenient and offer plenty of possibilities for achieving beautiful glazes and surfaces.

If you are considering buying a second-hand kiln, my advice is to avoid those built before the turn of the millennium. They are generally heavy and will use more energy. Make sure that the controller is included, as fitting a new one can be costly. The energy consumption is usually the limiting factor. If you are buying a kiln it is important to know if the kiln uses single phase (standard wall plug) or 3 phase (larger red plug) supply, and above all, the amperage (A) of your fuses. Electric kilns usually have a small plate on the side that gives the size of the kiln in litres (or cubic feet), maximum temperature and how many watts (W) it uses. If the amperage requirement is not included, it's possible to calculate this from the W and the number of phases: check with an electrician. Don't buy a kiln that is too large – for the beginner and the hobbyist it is both better and more fun to be able to fire regularly and often.

Low-firing techniques

The world of pottery is small and techniques from different countries will go on to have a new life in other parts of the world. One example is raku. The technique originates in Japan and is practised nowadays in a range of styles. What they all have in common is that they are fired at low temperatures (900–1000°C/1650–1800°F) and that the wares are removed from the kiln at the top temperature using tongs. The pots will be glowing when they come out and, surprisingly, they don't crack, as they are cooled down within minutes. The reason it works is mainly because the clay isn't sintered at these low temperatures, but if a pot is cooled down unevenly it will still crack easily. Traditionally, the pots were small with black or red glaze, but nowadays there are raku glazes in all colours. Raku glazes can be bought ready-made and can be coloured with oxides and stains. During cooling the pots are often put into sawdust, to reduce the clay (see page 135) so that it develops its characteristic black body.

The fact that the clay turns black when it comes into contact with organic materials (things that burn) can be exploited in many exciting ways. In horse-hair raku, potters draw and decorate directly onto the hot un-glazed clay with horse hair, feathers and similar. This leaves black marks with very sharp lines.

In Russian raku, obvara, the pots are quickly dipped into a mixture that resembles a watery sourdough. When the pot is taken out, the dough is baked and forms a vivid black and white pattern across the surface.

An older technique that makes the most of the clay turning black is smoke firing (also called pit firing). In modern versions of these firing techniques, bisque-fired pots are packed together with twigs and sawdust in a simple brick frame that is set alight. The areas where the pots haven't come into contact with air will turn matt black. With some skill it's also possible to fire non-bisque-fired pots this way. As long as your expectations are not too high for the first attempt, you can just dig a hole in your garden and try it out! Smoky but fun.

Building a small raku kiln is pretty straightforward and it can be made from accessible materials such as Leca blocks if you want to fire with wood. A raku barrel is also a relatively common kiln where the temperature is controlled using a gas torch. The raku barrel is made from an oil barrel lined with ceramic fibre.

High-firing techniques

Stoneware temperatures, on the other hand, place more requirements on the kiln. The kiln bricks have to be fireproof, and the kiln will need a larger firebox and chimney. It's tempting to make a small kiln, but the reality is that the smaller the kiln, the more unpredictable it will be when firing. The reason is that a larger kiln's mass and volume act as a buffer when you add wood.

There are also a range of firing techniques for stoneware kilns. Some people might be familiar with salt glazing, such as the red-black, shiny classic pots from Höganäs in Sweden. The technique probably developed 400–500 years ago in the region of present-day Germany, by firing ceramics with wood from discarded salt barrels. What happened was that the salt in the wood vaporized in the high temperature and formed a durable glass where it came into contact with the clay. Since salt barrels are scarce nowadays, we fire with standard wood and throw salt onto the wood to achieve the same effect. Salt-glazed wares have one of the most durable glazes that exist in ceramics. Until the arrival of plastic, salt-glazed pots were used a lot within industry, and they are well suited for all forms of utilitarian ware.

Standard table salt vaporizes and reacts with clay at temperatures above 1100°C (2010°F).

The workshop

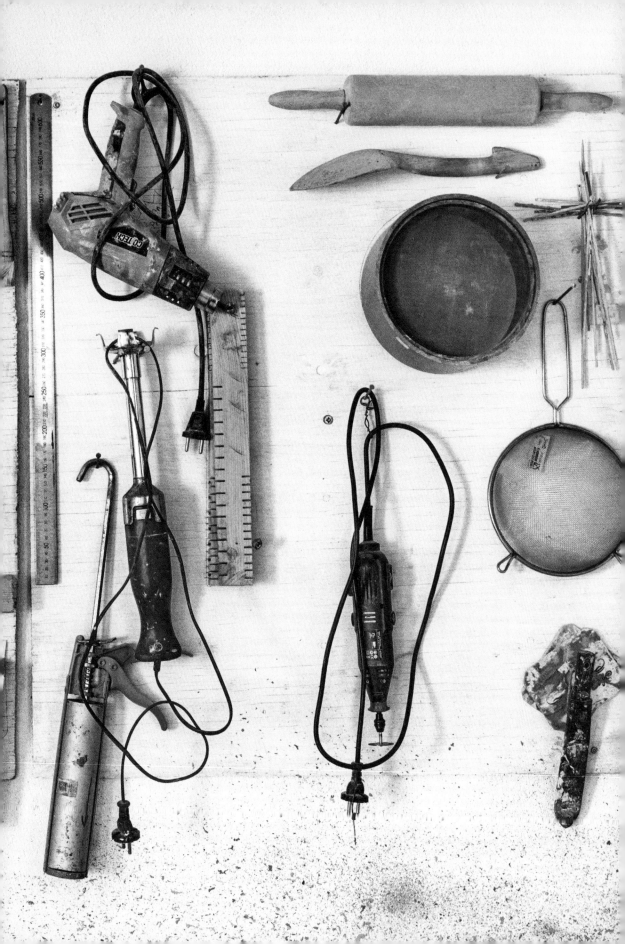

Workshop, atelier, studio or den – a favourite place, like a favourite child, has many names. If there's one thing I have learnt, it is that working with pottery can be carried out in many different ways and with very different goals and prerequisites. Below are some tips for how a workshop can be set up.

As with all handicrafts there are certain risks, and for potters the largest hazard is possibly our ingredients. They can be hazardous as dust or when they are burnt, but also if they are flushed out into the water supply. There is also an ethical aspect to consider. Some substances are mined under appalling conditions for humans in a way that is bad for the environment. Read up on the substances you use and gather information online with a critical eye. Throughout the decades, many persistent myths have evolved, and new ones pop up from time to time. Nowadays the ingredients are labelled with information about what we actually know about their risks.

You will probably need a sturdy table for wedging clay, but the disadvantage of a stationary table is that it will collect dust. By reducing the number of flat surfaces in a workshop it's easier to keep the dust at bay. Instead of permanent shelving you can put up brackets for loose shelves that can easily be moved around and cleaned off. With the help of a couple of trestles you also have a temporary table. Keep an eye on where in the workshop dust gathers and check if you can remove that surface, or the things on top of it. A few plastic crates with lids can be a good investment. One surface that can't be removed, however, is the floor. It's best if you can hose it down and scrape it to remove clay dust. If that isn't possible, a mop will do the job well. A brush or a vacuum cleaner are not good alternatives as they will stir up the fine dust that you want to avoid. If you breathe in too much clay dust you can develop pneumoconiosis, but as a hobbyist the risk is minimal. In that case, cleaning is more about creating a nice work space and avoiding other toxic substances that you might use in your practice. I decided early on to avoid most of the substances that can be hazardous and bad for my health. The glazes that I'm sharing in this book are, in my view, as safe and environmentally friendly as glazes can be.

Clay can easily block the drains, so it's a good idea to flush drains in the workshop liberally with water. It's of course preferable if the clay doesn't get in there in the first place. It can be prudent early on to fit your workshop with a sedimentation tank that sits between the sink and the drains, and makes sure that clay and other substances will settle at the bottom of the tank while the water drains off. A sedimentation tank is a simple construction that you can easily build yourself with some pipes and plastic crates or buckets. The idea

is to build a step system, where the water flows off from the surface and the heavier particles sink to the bottom in gradiated chambers until it's finally flushed out in the drains as clear water. Instead of a sedimentation tank you can also have a couple of buckets of water that you use for washing up, before rinsing under the tap. The accumulated residue from the buckets or the sedimentation basin will need to be emptied from time to time and should be disposed of at a household waste site. But the residue can also be reused, and if it's mainly glaze residue that you've got, it can be worth trying it as a glaze before discarding it. For years, potters have disposed of their residue by collecting it in a large bowl and firing it into a glass slab that can be used as a decorative object.

Avoid having the kiln in the same place that you work with clay, since some hazardous substances will be released during firing. Ideally, you should keep the kiln in its own separate room with a fan to extract the gases during firing. I have a bathroom fan that sits in an existing ventilation point in the room, but it would be even better if I had a hood connected to an extractor fan positioned over the kiln. An alternative is to place the kiln outdoors under a roof. As long as it's not exposed to rain and snow it won't get damaged.

The risk of fire is minimal when it comes to electric kilns, but insurance companies will impose certain safety restrictions (your insurance company should be able to advise). When the kiln is at top temperature, a good rule of thumb is to lightly touch any flammable materials (like wood) that are near. If the surfaces are so hot that you could burn yourself, there is a hazard. Move the kiln further away or install a heat shield in a non-flammable material.

←

A well-designed workshop will minimize the effort needed to carry out tasks. From that perspective, a large sink was a great investment for me, since it became easier to clean. Pictured here with some washing-up and a homemade mixer.

My tools

You can make most of the tools that are used in a pottery, and often, they will be superior to store-bought tools. You can make them more precise, they are cheaper, and often of better quality. Besides, it's a nice hobby to craft and create tools. The tools you use will play a fairly significant role in the final appearance of your pots, especially when you start getting a bit of flow in your production. It's not a bad idea to have a few alternatives to be able to express the personality of each pot.

Twisted cutting wire (2)

Store-bought cutting wires that are available to buy are often made from a fairly thick wire, which will just about do the job it's designed for. A thick wire will cause the clay to stick once you have cut it off the wheel, due to the wire being too smooth and thick. The advantage is that it's not as delicate as a thinner twisted wire, which shouldn't be folded since it will easily snap. The instructions here are to make a 20cm (8in) long cutting wire, but for plates you will need a longer one.

1. Chucks with sock for padding (see picture on page 114)
2. Twisted cutting wire
3. Compass
4. Measuring sticks with cutting wire
5. Homemade extruder gun
6. Bull's tongue
7. Wooden kidney
8. Throwing stick/egote
9. Sponge stick/diddler
10. Chamois leather
11. Sharp wooden stick
12. Fettling knife
13. Sponge
14. Wooden knife
15. Trimming tool
16. Large wooden throwing rib

MATERIALS
• Whittling knife
• Two wooden sticks, approximately 5cm (2in) long
• Pliers or heavy-duty scissors
• Stainless steel wire, 0.3—0.4mm (.012in)

Cut a notch at the centre of each stick and cut 40cm (16in) wire. Fold the wire in half and twist together at the ends. Attach a stick to each end of the double wire, twisting the wire round into place. Secure one of the sticks to a small piece of soft clay in the middle of the potter's wheel. Twist the whole wire by spinning the wheel while holding the other stick directly above the first. I usually keep rotating until there is 2mm (1/16 in) in between each twist.

Fettling knife (12)

For cutting clay it's good to have a fettling knife, a thin knife with a flexible blade. You can easily make your own from waste materials from your local DIY store. You will however need a bench grinder or other grinding machine to shape the blade.

MATERIALS
• Used steel cable tie, 17cm (7in)
• Bench grinder
• Fabric strips
• Masking tape

The first 7cm (2³⁄₄in) of the cable tie will become the blade and the rest will become the handle. Start by making the shape of the blade by using a bench grinder. My suggestion is that the blade is 10mm (1/2 in) at the base and 3mm (1/8 in) at the tip before it's immediately formed into a sharp point. Avoid grinding it too quickly, as the cable tie will quickly become very hot. Steel cable ties are generally so thin that you don't have to sharpen them to create an edge. Wrap the handle in fabric strips so that it becomes more comfortable to hold the knife. Secure into place with masking tape or a few tight knots.

Throwing stick/egote (8)

A throwing stick or an egote is a great tool for shaping the body of narrow-necked pots. Throwing sticks come in several different shapes that will help you reach inside, but a simple straight handle with a bump at the end will get you a long way. A small narrow 'head' is good for reaching down into narrow necks, while a wider larger 'head' will make it easier to shape soft curves and thin the clay further.

59

MATERIALS
- Piece of hardwood, approximately 4.5 x 25cm (1³⁄₄ x 10in) and 1cm (½in) thick
- Whittling knife
- Sandpaper in different grit sizes, for example 80, 150, 400
- Oil — linseed oil, cooking oil or similar

Sketch out the profile of the throwing stick on the piece of wood. Use the knife to whittle the shape. Make sure that you cut at the correct angle to avoid breaking off pieces of wood, and make sure you cut the wood with the grain. Once whittled into shape, sand the throwing stick with sandpaper. Place it in a plastic bag and add 50ml (3 tbsp) oil. Leave to stand overnight. If you sand the throwing stick after oiling it, you can get it really smooth. If you can't get hold of a cut piece of wood, it's usually possible to find a crooked piece of wood in the forest that you can whittle.

Trimming tool (15)

There are various makes of trimming tool but I still haven't found any that are as long-lasting as the ones I make myself. Besides, if I make one myself, I also get the opportunity to shape it to suit my own requirements. I usually buy different kitchen knives at flea markets, preferring to pick the ones with slightly thinner blades.

MATERIALS
- Permanent marker
- Stainless steel kitchen knife
- Bench grinder
- Small handheld gas torch
- Bucket of water
- Tongue-and-groove pliers or other pliers

Sketch out the profile of the trimming tool on the knife blade and grind into shape using a bench grinder. It's a good idea to make one side straight and one convex, and to have a range of different trimming tools with varying lengths on the cutting edge. Sharpen to create a cutting edge on both sides, from tip to a point beyond where you will bend the knife. When you are happy with the result, heat the area where the blade will be bent with a gas torch. When the metal glows orange it's ready to be shaped. Take hold with your pliers and bend the metal 90 degrees in one movement. You can heat it again if the result isn't satisfactory. Quickly place the hot part of the knife into a bucket of water. By cooling it down quickly, the metal will become harder and stay sharp for longer. If at a later date you feel that the trimming tool has become blunt, sharpen it using a bench grinder or a metal file.

Measuring sticks (4)

I use measuring sticks to cut uniform clay slabs. There are other techniques, such as rolling using a standard rolling pin or a slab roller, or by tossing to stretch it. Each method has its advantages. The advantage of using measuring sticks is that they will create less stress in the clay that can otherwise lead to cracks. The disadvantage is that it's not possible to cut very big slabs.

MATERIALS
- Two pieces of wood, 38 x 4.5cm (15 x 1³⁄₄in) and 2.5cm (1in) thick, preferably hardwood
- Two clamps or tape
- Ruler
- Pencil
- Saw, for example Japanese saw
- Coloured marker pen

Check that the pieces of wood

are fairly rectangular. Tape or clamp the two pieces together lengthwise so that you can measure and saw both pieces at the same time. Along one of the long sides, measure and mark 14 lines with a 5mm (¼in) gap in between each line. Be careful that the lines don't become wonky. Saw an 8-mm (½-in) deep groove at each line. This will make clay slabs that are just about 5mm (¼in) thick. I also mark every other line with a coloured marker so that it's easier to find the placement for the cutting wire when I work. By turning the clamped pieces, you can also make scores with different-sized gaps in between for making slabs with different thicknesses. I use a 30cm (12in) cutting wire with the measuring sticks, but I have replaced the sticks with two nuts which are less in the way when I'm using it. On page 88 you can see how the tool is used.

Homemade extruder gun (5)

An extruder gun is a quick and convenient tool for creating coils of clay with different forms. Larger commercial extruders can also be used for making hollow shapes and it is a really fun tool to use to make all kinds of ceramics. The extruder gun on page 58 is for the small jobs, such as handles or decorative coils. Personally, I mainly use it for making little jagged biscuits that I stack my ceramics on top of in the wood-fired kiln.

MATERIALS
• Applicator gun/sealant gun
   with cartridge for the clay
• Jar lids
• Metal drill
• Metal files

An applicator gun will rarely need any modification, but if it's possible, buy one made out of metal and it will be able to take the strain better. I have made a working extruder gun by combining parts from two broken ones, so ask your neighbours and keep an eye out at flea markets and you might be able to avoid buying one. Look for jar lids that will fit into the cartridge for your gun. In many cases there will be a gallery (or flange) that will hold the lid into place once the clay is added, as long as the lid fits inside. To make a template for a simple handle, take a 6mm (¼in) metal drill and drill two holes in the jar lid with a 15mm (¾in) gap in between. Then file down the gap in between. You might not necessarily have to make it completely straight, instead you can add notches and curves to create an interesting profile.

When using the extruder gun you will need soft clay. I also usually wet the inside of the extruder gun to reduce the friction. Place the templates that you have made from jar lids into the cartridge. Then roll a length of clay that can be inserted into the cartridge. Be careful to avoid air bubbles in the clay since they will pop when squeezed out through the templates. Squeeze out long coils of clay and then cut into pieces, as the two ends will usually be wonky and misshapen.

Black pot: Potclays Craft Crank clay, fired in a wood-fired kiln with reduction cooling (see page 138). White pot: Mixed clay with added fine sand, decorated with porcelain slip and fired in an electric kiln. Brown pot: Solargil natural clay 58310ST, fired in a wood-fired kiln with a little salt (see page 129). Light/beige pot: Cebex cs900, fired in a wood-fired kiln with oxidation cooling (see page 138).

FORMING TECHNIQUES

Throwing vases off the hump might not be the first technique you will try, but once you get to grips with the basics you will go on to learn how to collar the clay and use a throwing stick. Hold the throwing stick firmly with your left hand to bulge out the body. The right hand supports the top of the pot so that it doesn't wobble off centre.

>

On the potter's wheel

Anyone who wants to learn how to throw clay will soon realize that we have quite a lot of fingers that can push, pull and get in the way. Just as with any other handicraft it will take time for your body to learn the technique, and I recommend observing, copying and going back to the same source over and over again.

There are loads of variations on grips, but all skilled potters actually do the same thing with the clay. My recommendation is to learn one way to start off with. Once you feel confident you will easily be able to extend your repertoire of different grips by observing and copying other potters.

When throwing, each step builds on the previous one, and as you master each stage the ones that follow will become easier. If the centring of the clay isn't adequate it will be difficult to pull up the clay, and if your pull up is uneven it's difficult to shape the cylinder and so on.

Before you start throwing, the clay will need to be centred. The aim is to place the clay in the middle of the wheel, to even out it out and prepare it for throwing. The strength required for centring doesn't come from your arms but mainly from connecting your upper body with the clay. Sitting close to and slightly above the potter's wheel will help, as you can lean your body against the clay to put force into it. Also make sure that there is contact between your hands to offer more stability. If it seems impossible to centre a large lump of clay, practise the basics with a smaller one.

CENTRING THE CLAY

1. Place the lump of clay in the middle of the wheel. Make sure that the clay is even and rounded on the part that you place down against the wheel.

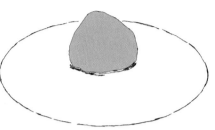

2. Pat the clay with both hands at the same time to centre it. Spin the potter's wheel slowly, or if the wheel allows, turn it as you pat. Keep patting until the clay is cone-shaped.

3. Increase the speed of the wheel. Wet your hands and clay as needed.

4. Support the left hand with your body and press down with your palm turned diagonally downwards and against the clay. The right hand supports the left and holds the clay.

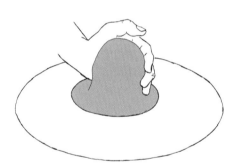

5. Place your left hand at the base of the clay and shape it into a cone. This will happen naturally when you angle the left palm slightly more upwards and lightly squeeze the clay. The right hand is placed on the opposite side and supports the clay.

6. Bend down the cone by folding the tip diagonally downwards. The right hand holds the clay closest to the wheel and counters any unevenness that can often appear at this stage.

7. Repeat steps 3, 4, 5 and 6 until the clay is a centred, forming an even and symmetrical squat cone.

69

TROUBLESHOOTING

- If you push the clay off the wheel, it's probably due to the pressure not being directed downwards enough. Press down more to keep the clay in place.
- If you get a pain in your wrist when centring, it's likely that you aren't pressing with the base of your palm. Move the pressure closer to your wrist.
- If you pull or twist off the tip of the clay, it's likely that you are pinching the clay between both hands – be careful to press mainly with one hand and relax the other when you see it starting to happen.

- If you can't pull the clay up from the bottom, use your little finger to press inwards at the base. The little finger is surprisingly strong, so try to bend it a little for a big effect.
- If the clay moves off-centre when you bend the cone downwards, it is probably because you are pressing it down too forcefully. What happens is, as the clay is pushed down onto the

wheelhead it is pushed out in an uncontrolled manner. Press more at the side and allow the clay time to find its own way down.
- If you end up with a bowl on the top of your clay when coning it, it is due to the cone being too flat at the top. Slide your thumb upwards to make the top more pointed during the whole coning movement.

Throwing a cylinder

Throwing clay can be a form of meditation, a way to produce quickly, and a competitive sport, but for me it's a way to create expressive pots. With that in mind the right technique, speed and perfection are less crucial, which can be quite liberating.

It's not uncommon for me to come across students who cannot throw higher than 15cm (6in). This is usually because they are trying to squeeze up the clay in between the inner and outer hand instead of pulling it up. A good pull of the clay is achieved by pushing out the wall with your inner hand followed by stretching the wall upwards.

At the start, focus on letting the outer hand lead the pulling, but when you use both hands it's possible to throw extra thinly. The pull will always come from the base of the pot, and as you get more experienced you will feel when the pull brings up clay with it. If you feel that the pull is no longer bringing the clay up, check you haven't changed the angle of your right hand. Don't be tempted to thin out the top of the pot in order to achieve more height until the very last stage of the pot's creation.

Water is needed when throwing but be careful not to use too much. Too much water will cause the clay to lose its stability and become tired. It is usually better to throw using the slurry (liquid clay) on your hands and add water to that if needed. Quick throwers can add water without causing any problems, but it's rarely a good start for the beginner.

How quickly you should pull up the clay depends on how quickly the potter's wheel rotates, and there aren't really any right or wrongs. As a rule, it's more difficult to control the clay when the potter's wheel spins too quickly but it's also difficult to get an even pull if it spins too slowly. Find the speed that works for you and practise to achieve even throwing lines (see page 72) where you pull the hands slowly in relation to the pottery wheel's rotation.

Aim for an evenly thick wall when you learn to throw. An even wall can be pulled up more and is easier to shape. That said, that tiny irregularity in a throwing line or kink in the shape can be a source of personality and liveliness.

71

THROWING A CYLINDER

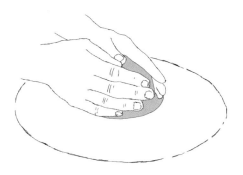

1. Cup the clay with both hands and make a hole with both thumbs. The thumbs should be touching.

2. Change your grip and pull the base towards you from inside. Shape the clay into a ring that is slightly wider than you want the cylinder to be.

3. Press the base down a couple of times to avoid s-cracks during the drying process (see page 33). Check the thickness of the base with a needle tool, plunging the needle in and sliding your finger down until it touches the clay and pulling it out again without shifting finger position. The base should be around 5mm (¼in) thick.

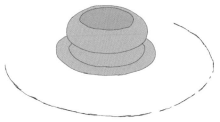

4. Grip the ring that you have made using a claw grip (as shown). Keeping the claw grip, hold the clay firmly in your hand to centre any irregularities.

5. Pull the clay into a cone shape using the claw grip. In a claw grip, you pull the clay by placing the thumb underneath the clay ring and pushing it upwards and inwards.

6. Pull the clay into a cylinder using a French grip. In a French grip, you place the left hand on the inside of the cylinder and push out a bump using your ring and middle finger. With your right hand, you lift and stretch this bump on the outside using the knuckle on your index finger.

7. Towards the end of the pull, the right and left hands will come closer together.

8. Gently compress the rim with your fingers and centre it if necessary. Release the cylinder slowly while the wheel spins, so that you don't pull it off centre.

9. If necessary, you can collar the cylinder by using the three-point grip. The three-point grip is a squeezing grip using both hands around the cylinder. Work from the bottom up. Support the cylinder at the top using your index fingers.

10. Pull up once or twice using the French grip.

11. Trim off any excess clay at the base with a wooden knife or turning tool. Make a notch at the base to help direct the cutting wire.

12. Remove the cylinder using a cutting wire while the potter's wheel spins. The wire will need to be taut and pulled through in just under one rotation of the wheel.

TROUBLESHOOTING

- If you're not getting enough clay from the base when using the claw grip, it is generally because you haven't pushed enough with your thumb. Since the clay is thick at this stage, you can often use more force than you might think in order to shape a clear bump that you can pull.

- If you're not getting enough clay from the base when applying the French grip, it can usually be solved by gathering clay before you start to pull it up. Apply your grip right down by the base, but once you have pushed out your interior hand and it is ready to pull, wait for five rotations of the wheel before you start. If you have a good grip, clay will gather above the right knuckle that you can pull up.

- If you tear the cylinder or if it gets too thin, it is generally because you haven't got enough clay from the base and have overcompensated later on by pulling up too much. Practise pulling up the clay from the base and let go when you feel that the clay gets too thin higher up.

- If the clay gets twisted and torn as you pull it up, it may be because you are pinching the clay. Increase the distance in height between your hands and/or add a little water to lessen the friction.

- If the cylinder doesn't come up straight but flares out at the top, it is likely that you are leaning your right arm against your knee during throwing. Make sure to pull your arm away from the knee as the cylinder grows.

- If the clay flops over the right hand when you pull it, you need to lift the bump more with your left hand and straighten up the clay into a more vertical position with your right hand.

- If you are left-handed, I advise you to work with the same hand positions as those who are right-handed. When you throw, both hands are active and alternately driving, and the problems won't be avoided by mirroring the grip.

- If you get a lot of water in the bottom of the cylinder you can remove this by using a little sponge attached to a stick. If you use more slurry and less water when throwing, this won't usually be necessary.

$\longrightarrow$
Failed form and glaze experiments are gathered in the garden. In order to make good pots you need to make bad ones — that's true for me at least.

Throwing a plate

It's fairly easy to accidentally end up with plates on the potter's wheel, but making plates in a controlled way can take a few attempts. A plate is made up of a well where the food is placed, and a rim around the outside that frames the food or that can be used as a surface for decorating.

Throwing bats

I throw most of my plates on a bat to avoid bending or misshaping them. The bat can be attached in various ways and on many modern wheels there are holes that can be used to secure them with a couple of bolts. Potters are a creative bunch, but the most important thing is that the bat itself doesn't cause any problems when you're making plates. So choose a solution that works for you.

MATERIALS
• I used about 1kg (2lb) French
  clay 58310ST (0–0.5 grog) from
  Solargil for this plate. I
  always try to work with a soft
  clay for plates.
• Throwing rib
• Cutting wire
• Trimming tool
• Chamois leather
• Throwing bat, in this case a
  19mm (¾ in) particle board
  with a diameter of 30cm (12in)
• Needle tool

ATTACHING A BAT WITH CLAY

1. Centre a scant kilogram (around 2lb) of clay on the wheel.

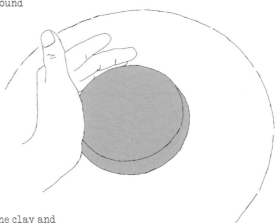

2. With your left hand, hold the clay and lean the edge of the clay inwards.

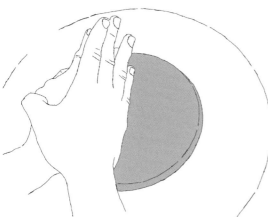

3. Using the side of your right hand, gradually pull out the clay from the middle towards your stomach. The left hand leans the edge inwards to prevent slurry and air getting trapped underneath the growing 'plate'. The plate should be three-quarters of the size of the bat's diameter.

4. Open up a hole in the middle and create grooves at regular intervals in the width of the plate. Aim to create grooves that are rounded and of an even depth.

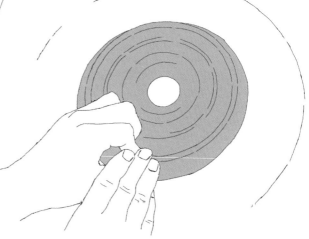

79

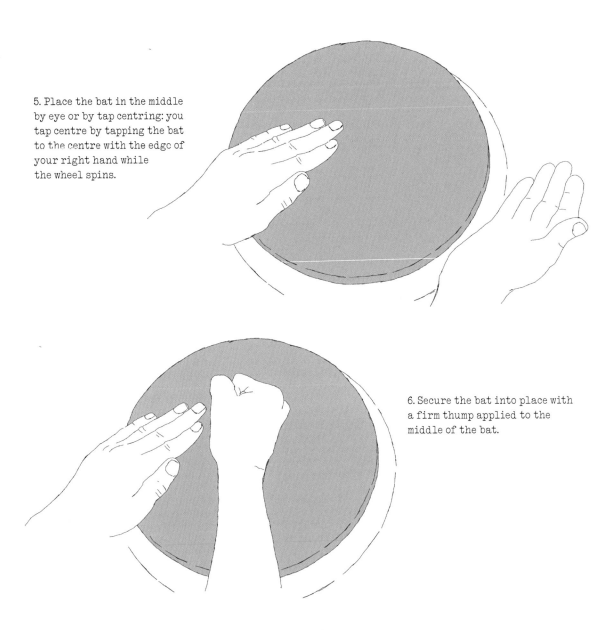

5. Place the bat in the middle by eye or by tap centring: you tap centre by tapping the bat to the centre with the edge of your right hand while the wheel spins.

6. Secure the bat into place with a firm thump applied to the middle of the bat.

TROUBLESHOOTING

- If the bat is uneven, with one side higher than the other, you can level it out with another thump a couple of centimetres away from the centre. Don't be tempted to thump the edge of the bat as it will wobble even more.

- If you can't spread the clay out from the centre, it's usually that you haven't been able to bring enough clay from the centre. Push the edge of your hand down into the middle of the clay and pull the ridge towards you, avoiding sliding over it.

- Tap centring can take time to master. Time the taps so that you are tapping on the side that sticks out. If the bat gets stuck too quickly, wet the clay underneath so it dries slower. Place your left hand on top so it doesn't slide off as you tap.

THROWING A PLATE

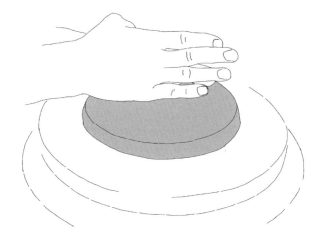

1. Centre the clay.

2. Using the edge of your right hand, gradually pull out the clay from the middle towards your stomach. Using your left hand, lean the edge inwards to avoid slurry and air getting trapped underneath the growing plate.

3. Place your hands on top of each other and open up the clay in the middle using your index and middle fingers.

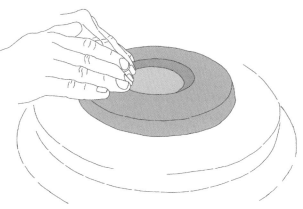

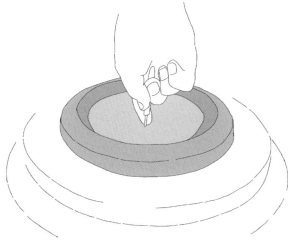

4. Pull the clay straight towards you in one or two pulls so that you get an outer ring of clay and a level base in the middle.

5. Check the thickness of the base with a needle tool. The base should be 5mm (¼in) plus the height of the foot ring (if you intend to have one).

6. If needed, press the base down with a throwing rib. Hold the rib at an angle with both hands.

7. Centre the outer ring using a firm claw grip and pull the wall straight upwards. Read about the claw grip on page 72.

8. If you want, pull the wall up further using a French grip. Read about the French grip on page 73.

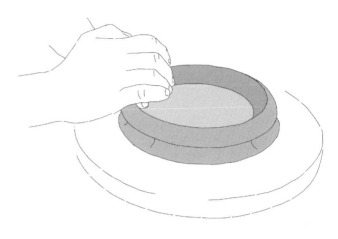

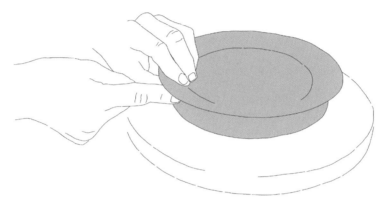

9. Fold the plate's edge down with your left hand and support it underneath with your right hand.

10. Press and shape the rim using chamois leather.

11. Make a score line close to the bat with a turning tool.

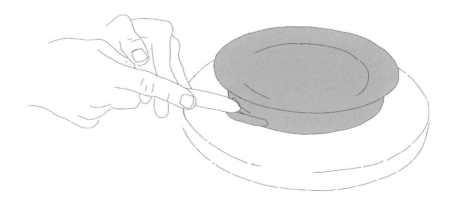

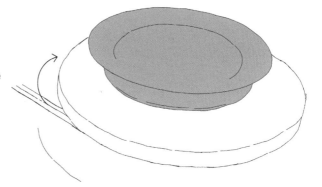

12. Cut underneath the plate with a taut cutting wire.

13. Remove the bat from the wheel using a tool such as a large foot shaper.

TROUBLESHOOTING
- If the bat becomes loose when you centre the clay it's usually because the angle the pressure is coming from is incorrect. Press downwards more to keep the bat in place.

- If the bat slides, it can be due to too much moisture in between the bat and the clay underneath. You will need to adapt the amount of water depending on the material of your bat.
- If the rim starts to wobble it

generally doesn't have enough support underneath. Leave more clay underneath the rim that you can trim off later. Make sure that you are only supporting (not pushing) the rim with your right hand during shaping.

Trimming and glazing a plate

Once the plate has been thrown, I leave it on the bat until the clay is leather hard, which usually takes around a day. Sometimes I have to slow down the drying process so that the plate doesn't dry too quickly at the rim before the base dries. For this I usually use plastic or an old sheet.

It's quick to trim this kind of plate. Remove the excess clay from the sides and a couple of millimetres from the base to create a low foot ring on the plate. Don't trim the plate too soon, instead wait until the base is leather hard, this way you minimize the risk of the base collapsing. I leave this kind of plate to dry right side facing up, since the base will easily collapse if it is flipped upside down to achieve a more even drying. Often I'm able to raw glaze the day after trimming.

Pressing a plate

Using a press mould might be one of the easiest ways to make flatware (flat objects). Once the press mould is made, it's possible to produce a large number of uniform objects fairly quickly.

Press moulds

You can easily make a press mould from a lump of clay but remember that what you form will be the interior shape. Press moulds can be made from a range of different materials. In my workshop I use unfired clay for rounder forms and wood when I'm looking to create something more angular. To make wooden moulds I use a mitre saw and sandpaper. For clay moulds I use a knife, kidney and possibly a cardboard template. It's better if you make the press mould from an absorbant material but it's not essential. So it would probably be possible to make interesting press moulds using a 3D printer, for example.

To make the press mould in the picture, see right, I cut out two oval templates, one for the top and one for the bottom. I placed these on the top and bottom of a piece of solid clay that I had carefully cut to the height of the final plate. By then cutting in between the two templates, I got a rough form that I left to dry until leather hard before hollowing out until the walls were around 3cm (1¼in) thick. I took the opportunity to shape handles in the carved-out area to ensure the press mould could easily be lifted out when used. Finally, I went over the surface with a kidney to smooth the edges. The press mould can be used once it's bone dry.

If you are working with an exact template, you should note that both the mould and the plate will shrink. To compensate for the shrinkage, you can add 15–20 per cent to the template's measurements.

You can recycle failed or unused press moulds made from clay together with other waste from the workshop.

MATERIALS
- Clay, preferably with grog. For the plate pictured I used Goerg & Schneider 596 (40% 0–1.5mm grog). The clay turns a nice brown-red colour in my wood-fired kiln and the coarse grog gives a lively surface.
- Cutting wire
- Measuring sticks made from wood (5mm/¼ in gaps)
- Foam from an old mattress (at least 10cm/4in thick)
- Flexible kidney (can be bought or cut out of an old credit card)
- Wheat flour
- Tea strainer
- Unfired clay press mould
- Knife with a thin, flexible blade

PRESSING A PLATE

1. Shape 5kg (11 lb) clay into a rectangle. It's fine to take the clay straight from the packet and bash it into an even shape that will give you slabs to the required size.

2. Using a cutting wire and measuring sticks, cut out around ten slabs from the clay. Hold the wire taut and push the measuring sticks firmly down towards the table. I prefer to cut the slab at the bottom first and then work my way up from there, moving the cutting wire one step up on the measuring sticks for each pull.

3. Carefully lift the top slab, transfer it to the foam and smooth it out on both sides with a flexible kidney.

4. Sprinkle a thin layer of flour over the clay using a tea strainer to make sure the clay doesn't stick to the press mould during the next stages.

5. Press down the press mould in the middle of the clay slab (on top of the foam). Press until the whole mould is pushed down into the foam.

6. With one hand holding the press mould, roughly trim off any clay that protrudes above the edge.

89

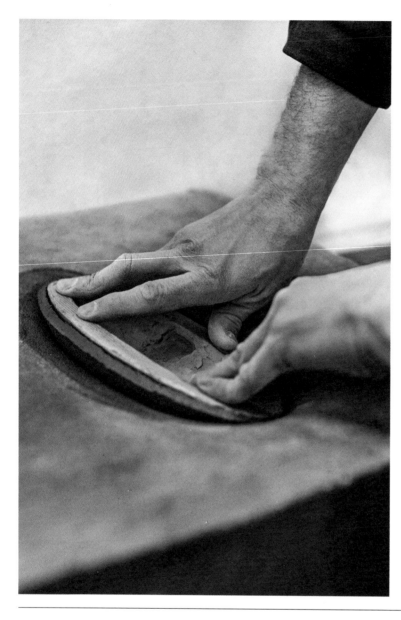

7. Once the edge has been trimmed, press and wiggle the mould against the sides to make sure the clay is shaped properly around the mould.

8. Neatly trim the edge. Make sure to keep the knife blade at the same angle all the way around to make it even.

9. Lift the plate, together with the press mould, onto a board, where you will leave the plate to dry, then lift out the press mould and leave the plate standing on the board.

An interesting way to develop this technique further is to make patterns on the press mould, to use different plaster moulds or to add handles and feet once the plate has dried a little. To attach handles and feet, score the surface with a tool and apply a bit of slip in between the plate and whatever you are attaching.

TROUBLESHOOTING
• If the long sides of the plate drop outwards try using a slightly harder clay, but for some moulds you might have to push in the edges a little once the mould has been removed.
• If your plates crack during the drying or firing process, I recommend trying a different clay. Cracks are caused by tensions in the object owing to the clay having been bent or folded during production. Clays have different sensitivities to this and with experience you will learn how to avoid this happening.
• If the clay sticks together when you cut the slabs, try using a harder clay or a twisted cutting wire, as described on page 58.
• If the plate warps during firing, it's usually due to a problem in the forming process. Thinner shapes and certain clays, such as porcelain, are more prone to warping than others. A simple solution is to make the plate a little thicker or just use a different clay.

90

Handles

Jugs have probably been a staple commission for the potter throughout history and there is a rich tradition of forms and handles. It takes time to learn to pull handles, so a good tip is to start adding handles to your wares early on so that both techniques develop simultaneously.

The perfect handle

It is not unusual that a perfectly shaped pot doesn't go with any hande. As soon as you start throwing you will need to start thinking of where the handle should start and finish and adjust the handle and the body to fit each other.

To make it practical, a handle has to be comfortable to hold, so avoid sharp edges and handles that are too thin. When it comes to jugs it is important to think about balance, once the jug is filled with liquid. If the hand that holds the handle ends up too high up it can be heavy to pour, and if it ends up too low, the jug can easily become unstable and wobbly. The distance between the hand and the jug is also relevant for how heavy it is. It is easiest when the handle is positioned very close to the body of the jug, but there must of course be enough space for the hand as well as harmony with the design. That the handle needs to work from a practical point of view is sometimes forgotten during the design process, but if you want your objects to actually be used, practicality is key. The best handles sit well and feel natural in the hand.

Careful consideration is also important when you are adding a handle to a cup, especially when making sure that the person who drinks something hot from the cup won't suffer any burns. Personally, I want my coffee cups to be balanced with a smooth handle that makes it easy to drink the coffee. It is best to look at and test out different kinds of jugs and cups to figure out which kind you like the best.

Most of my handles are pulled directly onto the jug, but you can also choose to pull the handle fully and leave it to firm up before you attach it. The latter alternative might seem easier, but there is a directness and a liveliness in a handle that is pulled directly from the jug that is difficult to achieve in any other way. A good alternative to pulling handles is to use an extruder to easily create handles of different shapes. It is very efficient, but you will get a different kind of handle using this method. Choose themethod depending on the feel you are after.

```
MATERIALS
• Clay: I used Potclays 1102
   (6% fine grog), which gives a
   lovely rustic finish in my
   wood-fired kiln at the same
   time as sintering well.
• Sponge
• Towel
• Bowl of water
```

The body of the jug

I usually throw a jug's body the day before attaching the handle, using 1.5kg (3lb 5oz) of clay. For this design it is important to save clay at the top to be able to make the defined lip. I pull the spout up and fold it out before I lift the jug off the wheel. Spouts can be made in many different ways, but this way they get a bit of height and the generous character that suits the feeling that I'm after. The clay has a 'memory', so I will need to exaggerate the shape of the spout a little since the clay will retract into the shape it was thrown in as it dries.

Once I can lift the jug without it becoming misshapen, I lift it and push up the middle of the base a little by patting it. By doing this, I minimize the risk of the base bulging out in the middle after firing, which would cause the jug to wobble. I make sure that the body is leather hard before attaching the handle. Often I will need to place plastic over the jugs to prevent them drying out too much at the top, while I wait for the base to dry.

SHAPING THE LIP

1. Pull up the clay between the thumb and the index finger. Using a lot of water to make sure your hands don't stick, make the lip thin and even.

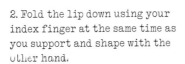

2. Fold the lip down using your index finger at the same time as you support and shape with the other hand.

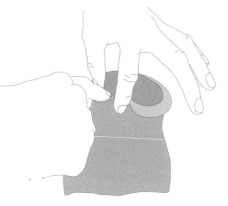

95

PULLING A HANDLE

1. Shape a lump of clay into a
cone and grip the wide end with
one hand.

2. Wet the palm of your hand and
pull along the shape with a light
squeezing movement. Alternate
pulling on the right-hand and
left-hand sides with a wet hand
to make the clay longer without
it becoming asymmetrical.

3. Divide the clay into several
smaller pieces by cutting them off
against the edge of your table.
For the jug in the picture, a coil
that is 8cm (3in) long and 4cm
(1½in) thick will work well.

4. Take one of the smaller pieces
and press one end against the
table to make it wider and
slightly convex. Add a drop of
water where you are attaching
the handle to the jug.

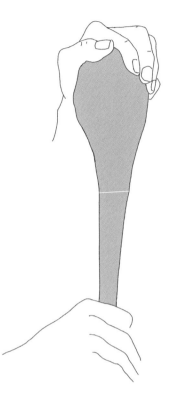

5. Press the shaped end of the
handle against the body. Smooth
out the handle towards the body
to create a seamless joint between
the two parts.

6. Hold the bottom half of the jug with one hand and start pulling the handle with the other hand. Use a lot of water on the hand that is pulling and alternate working from the right-hand and the left-hand sides to make a symmetrical handle.

7. Continue to pull the handle until you've got the required form and thickness. It is customary that the handle
gets thinner towards the lower joint, but with some practice you could, for example, pull handles that are at their thinnest in the middle.

97

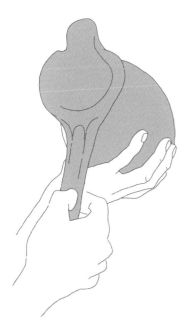

8. Run your thumb down the middle to make a decorative groove and bevel the edges with your thumb and index finger to create a handle in the same vein as shown.

9. Bend the handle inwards and attach it at the bottom with a little push. Pinch off any excess handle material. Don't let the jug stand up until the handle is attached at the bottom, since it will easily fall down and lose its shape.

10. Finetune the attachment at the bottom by rubbing out any excess clay with a wet thumb.

11. Add a drop of water to the lower joint and clean off any mess with a damp sponge.

12. When the handle is no longer sticky, cover the jug with plastic. Leave to stand until the handle and the body are evenly dry. Remove the plastic and leave the jug to dry slowly for a couple of days.

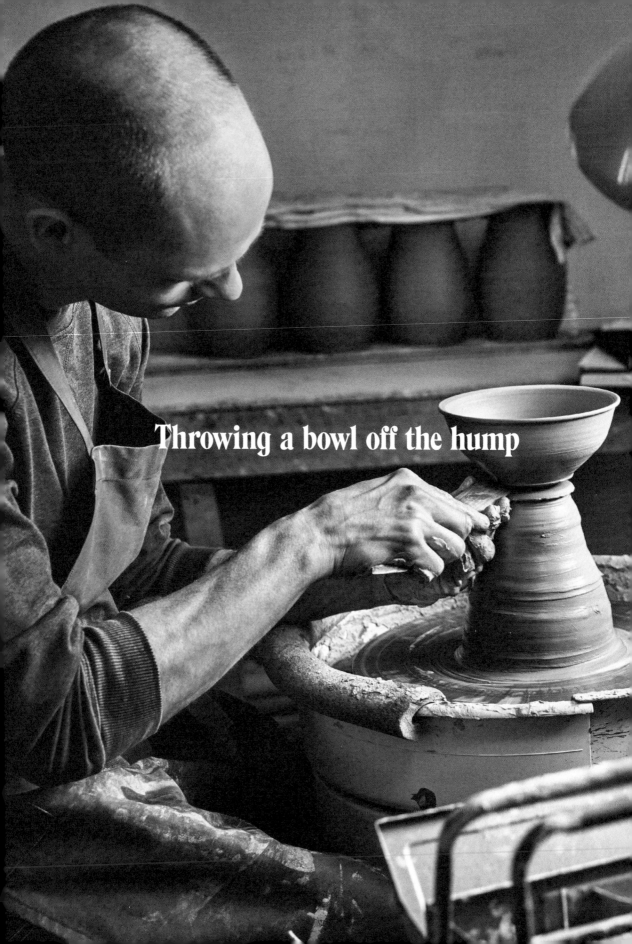

Throwing a bowl off the hump

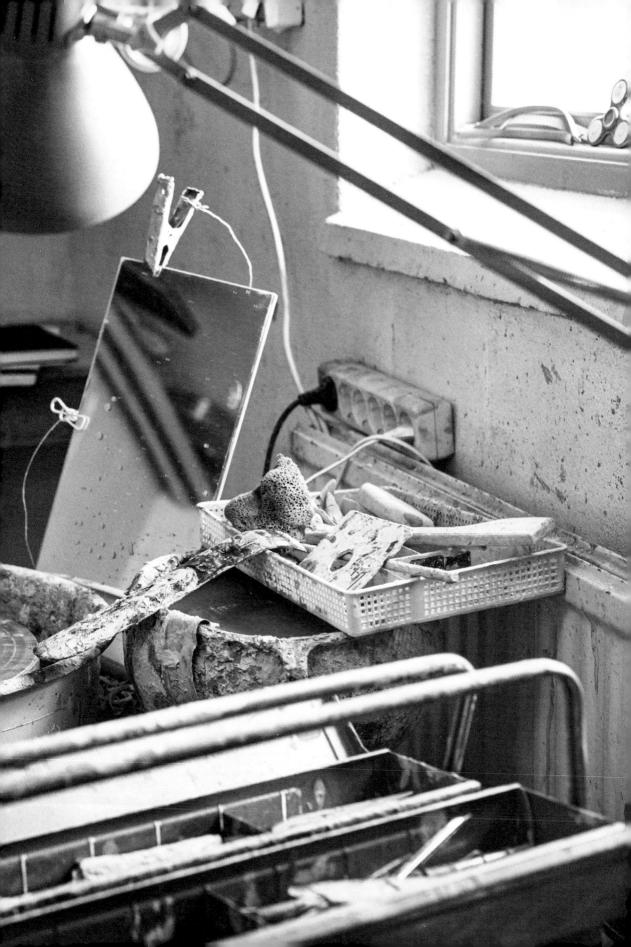

Throwing off the hump is a great way to make bowls, vases and other shapes with a foot ring. In practice it means that you only throw the upper part of the clay. When done successfully, it feels like bowls and jugs flow out into their forms and that potter and clay are the best of friends.

The hump underneath

When throwing off the hump you don't have to centre all the clay, only the part that you're working with. For each bowl, you bring up a bit more clay from underneath until you have used it all up. To make things easier, it's best not to make the clay too wide at the base, but instead aim to get a bit of height with the clay. The opportunity to add height to the clay is one of the main advantages with this technique, as it means that you can reach the underside of the design. In standard throwing it's difficult to reach the underside since the potter's wheel gets in the way. Many people also find that it gets easier to pull the clay from the base when throwing off the hump.

MATERIALS
- Clay, preferably a plastic clay with fine grog. I used Potclays 1110 (11% 0.2–0.4mm grog). It keeps its shape well and reacts easily with wood ash.
- Bull's tongue or a thick throwing rib
- Measuring stick (a ruler, caliper or a dragonfly tool)
- Chamois leather
- Wooden knife
- Cutting wire

THROWING A BOWL OFF THE HUMP

1. Pull up a cone from the clay.

2. Centre the upper part and make it the same width as you want the foot ring on the finished bowl to be.

3. Press down with your right thumb while holding the remaining fingers around the clay. Adjust how much clay you will pull up by varying how far you push your thumb down.

4. Pull out the base with your right thumb and at the same time, pinch lightly underneath the form with your left hand. Compress the clay at the base from the inside out a couple of times with the tip of your thumb.

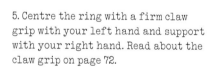

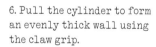

5. Centre the ring with a firm claw grip with your left hand and support with your right hand. Read about the claw grip on page 72.

6. Pull the cylinder to form an evenly thick wall using the claw grip.

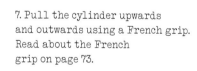

7. Pull the cylinder upwards and outwards using a French grip. Read about the French grip on page 73.

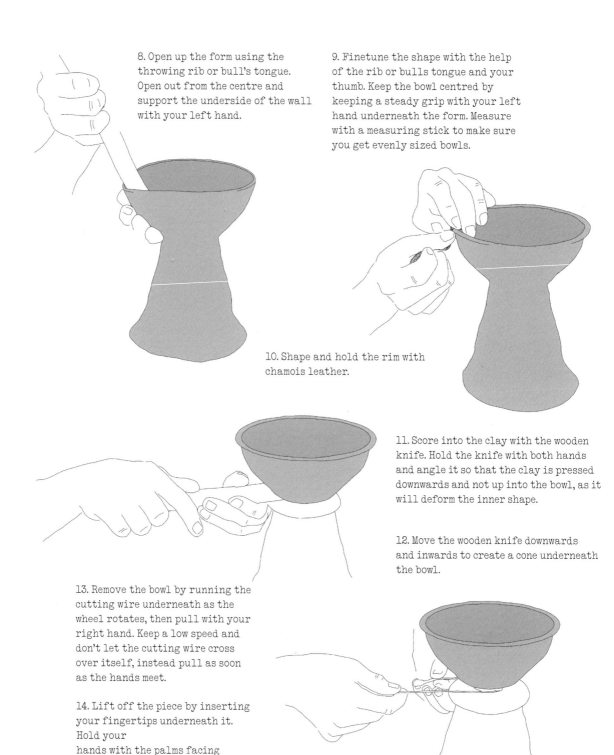

8. Open up the form using the throwing rib or bull's tongue. Open out from the centre and support the underside of the wall with your left hand.

9. Finetune the shape with the help of the rib or bulls tongue and your thumb. Keep the bowl centred by keeping a steady grip with your left hand underneath the form. Measure with a measuring stick to make sure you get evenly sized bowls.

10. Shape and hold the rim with chamois leather.

11. Score into the clay with the wooden knife. Hold the knife with both hands and angle it so that the clay is pressed downwards and not up into the bowl, as it will deform the inner shape.

12. Move the wooden knife downwards and inwards to create a cone underneath the bowl.

13. Remove the bowl by running the cutting wire underneath as the wheel rotates, then pull with your right hand. Keep a low speed and don't let the cutting wire cross over itself, instead pull as soon as the hands meet.

14. Lift off the piece by inserting your fingertips underneath it. Hold your hands with the palms facing up — this makes it easier to put the bowl down.

106

TROUBLESHOOTING

- If you get s-cracks in the base you probably need to trim the base more to get it thinner. You can avoid a lot of problems by compressing the clay more with your fingers as you open up the clay.
- If you get a fold on the inside of the bowl over the foot ring, it is usually because you have made the base too flat when you opened it up. Make a clear dip in the base from the start and focus on perfecting the centre before you open up the rest of the bowl.
- If the form collapses outside the hump it is usually because you have pressed downwards with your inner hand. Try to press outwards from the middle.
- If it starts to wobble when you open up the form, it is usually because you have pressed the bowl shape inwards. Try to only press the bowl shape outwards and don't be tempted to push it in from the outside.
- If the rim tears when you open up the bowl, next time use chamois leather to compress the rim at an earlier stage.
- If the bowl warps as you lift it off, try to score higher and deeper with your wooden knife. Your fingers should fit into the score and be able to reach right underneath the bowl.

$\leftarrow$

If you can throw a bowl off the hump you can also throw a cup, and if you learn how to collar the clay into a neck you can throw a vase. See the image on page 66 for tips on how to shape a vase.

Making marks in the form with your fingers or a tool is an effective way to create variation in your cups. You can even make the cups oval or square by pinching them in different ways. If you want to make sure they stay round however, you must re-centre the rim after you have made your marks. A glaze that moves during firing and gathers in the dips will enhance the design and make the body and glaze seem more integrated.

Note that I have shaped the cup's underside as well, and that the width of the foot ring is fairly close to the finished cup. This way it's easier to trim, since you know roughly how thick the base is.

Small cups thrown off the hump.

Trimming

Trimming off clay on a leather-hard piece is also called turning. You can do this to carve a foot ring, smooth the outside, and you can even refine the insides of bowls and plates. A foot ring contributes a lot to the feel of the finished piece, and there are many aesthetic choices that can make a bowl light, heavy, sturdy, subtle or – if you like – distinct.

Trimming tools

When trimming you need tools to cut with. In Korea, the use of a bent bamboo strip goes back a long way, while many potters today buy ribbon tools and other steel tools. Any trimming tool will do the job, but the harder the clay, the more important it is to use sharp tools to make the work easier. Regardless of the trimming tool you use, you will need to remember that you need to cut the clay off, not scrape it off. The latter will easily lead to misshapen bases and lost pots. Try holding the trimming tool at different angles to find a good position where the clay is trimmed off without the need for pressing down too much. On page 60 I describe how you can make a trimming tool which is also useful during the throwing process.

MATERIALS
- Foam
- Trimming tools, one smaller and one larger
- Compass
- Clay: I use a recycled clay mixture with a little added grog

←

In order not to damage the vase on the hard chuck I have covered the chuck with an old sock.

Tap centring

I usually trim bowls and plates placed on a piece of foam that I secure to the potter's wheel with a little slip. The foam makes sure that the rim doesn't get damaged and helps to keep the bowl in place if I just hold it with one hand. You can also secure the bowl directly to the potter's wheel using a few coils of clay or some water.

It's best to place pieces with high-sided shapes on a clay cone to trim them. This is called a chuck, and you can make it from clay when you need it. I use recycled clay for my chucks. Depending on the shape, the chuck can hold the shape through contact from the outside or the inside – the most important thing is that the shape is secured in place when you push it lightly downwards.

Regardless of method, it is a great help if you can learn to centre the pot using tap centring. With this technique it is quick to centre and particularly to re-centre if the pot ends up off-centre. Personally, I thought that creating foot rings was a devil of a job until the day I learned to tap centre.

Decide from the beginning which part you should centre, since thrown pots are rarely completely symmetrical. Be meticulous but don't go over the top: a slight margin of error won't be visible once the pot is finished. Trial and error is key to learning tap centring – make it a habit to have a few attempts every time you sit at the wheel.

You can practise tap centring using a pot that has already been fired. Place the pot as close to the centre as you can and place your left hand lightly onto the base. While the potter's wheel spins, tap the pot towards the centre using your right hand. Try to time it so that you are tapping the protruding part while you coax the pot towards the centre with your left hand.

TRIMMING A BOWL

1. Centre the bowl.

2. Level out 1cm (½in) in the middle that you will then use as the starting point.

3. Mark the width of the foot ring using a compass.

4. Trim off the outer part of the foot ring using a corner of your trimming tool. Your left hand holds the shape in place with index or middle finger. Trim off a little bit of clay at a time to remove any irregularities in stages.

5. Hold the bowl down with your left index or middle finger and remove clay until the foot ring has the required height. Steady your hands by keeping them in contact with each other.

6. Trim off the middle until the foot ring has the required height. The left hand holds the bowl in place by holding the foot ring.

7. Trim off the inside of the foot ring in stages. Start by carving out a small hole in the middle with the edge of the bull's tongue. Using the hole as a starting point, trim off the clay working outwards. This way you avoid pressing downwards against the thinning base.

8. Make sure that the maximum thickness of the base is 5mm (¼in). You can do this by pulling the bowl up and measuring it in between your fingers, or by lightly pressing down with your finger on the base to feel the resistance of the clay. You can also tap the base and thin it out until it sounds like a drum skin. Sometimes I think when the thickness is right it sounds like a hollow tree.

9. Smooth out the outside, and inside if needed, using a wider tool to minimize tool marks and refine longer curves.

← You can vary the appearance of the foot ring by using different trimming tools.

TROUBLESHOOTING

- If the trimming tool begins to chatter and leaves a rhythmic mark on the bowl, reduce the pressure and lower the speed on the wheel. Remove just the slightest amount of clay at a time until the marks disappear
- If you have difficulty getting a level base, lower the speed of the wheel and remove less clay on each rotation of the wheel. Gradually the base will level out as long as you can keep the trimming tool still.
- If you distort the base when trimming, it is generally because you have pressed down too much. Cut more outwards than downwards by making a dip in the middle and then trimming off the clay outwards from that point.
- If you get s-cracks in the base you may need to trim it thinner. A clay with more grog can lower the risk of cracking, as can taking steps to dry the bowl more evenly, like by covering it with fabric or plastic.

117

BUILDING A KILN

A *pytteugn* ('tiny kiln') is a small and fast-firing kiln suitable for those who want to start making their own wood-fired pottery. To build the kiln you will need about 240 firebricks. The kiln will take just under a day to build according to my plans. With a bit of thought it can easily be modified to become a raku kiln or be sized up if that's what you want.

As a rule, a wood-fired kiln has three distinct parts: a firebox where the wood is fed in and gets burned, a chamber where the pots are stacked, and a chimney that sucks air into the firebox by creating a through-draught. There are many types of kiln, but in the *pytteugn*, the firebox is placed underneath the chamber and the chimney, which makes it very efficient at reaching stoneware temperature.

Building a kiln isn't difficult, but there are three basic things that you need to know. Firstly, you will need to lay the bricks in a bond, which means that every new brick layer should overlap the gaps from the previous layer. I do it as best as I can in my brick-by-brick plan on page 124, but if you are building a small kiln, you may have to break this rule from time to time.

Secondly, you should check the measurements after each layer (or course, as it's called when you are laying bricks), and adjust to make sure the outer measurements are even. Use a spirit level to check that the construction is both level and vertically aligned. Take extra care to measure the two diagonals from corner to corner – if they are different it means that the kiln is skewed and that you will have to adjust the walls. Adjust the bricks by tapping them into position. Tapping the bricks against a straight plank works well for evening out the brickwork.

Thirdly, you will need very little or no mortar in between the bricks. This is called laying the bricks dry. If it's uneven or a bit too low in places, you can add standard slip to level it out. Using clay for the joints means that the bricks will be easy to clean and reuse in the future. You might be used to the wide mortar joints in a brick house, but that wouldn't work well for a kiln since all the bricks will move when the temperature increases. Any smaller gaps can be sealed with clay and sand during the firing.

Firebricks

If you intend to use the kiln for stoneware you will need to build it using firebricks that can withstand high temperatures. There are many different makes and sizes. In my brick-by-brick plan I have used a standard brick that measures 23 x 11.5 x 6.5cm (9 x 4½ x 2½in). If you get hold of bricks that differ by a couple of centimetres either way you can probably still use the same plan. Your kiln will end up with slightly different measurements when it's finished, but you will still have a working kiln.

There are two categories of firebricks: hardbricks and softbricks. Hardbricks are heavier, harder and more durable. Softbricks insulate better and are lighter. Most bricks will be labelled on the side, which means that you can easily look up information online if you want to know more. If you have the choice, I suggest that you build your kiln from softbricks, since it will make firing quicker. Besides, it means you will have fewer things to consider as you build, which can be a relief if this is your first kiln. You can buy bricks from distributors of fire-retardant materials, and you can sometimes get hold of bricks cheaply second hand. Buying bricks from a standard hardware store will usually be double the price.

You will also need a few half-bricks for your build. Softbricks are easy to saw with a standard handsaw, while hardbricks will require a bit more work to split. It is possible to saw them with a diamond cutting disc, but I suggest that you cut them with a brick hammer instead. To get a good cut, draw a line around the brick where you want it to split and then hammer repeatedly along the line. Once you have a shallow score in the brick you can apply more force and the brick will split along the score. Remember to protect your eyes with a pair of goggles as you do this.

$\longrightarrow$

At the top of the picture are soft firebricks with hard firebricks underneath. Since the bricks are a part of the chimney, I haven't bothered to seal the gaps.

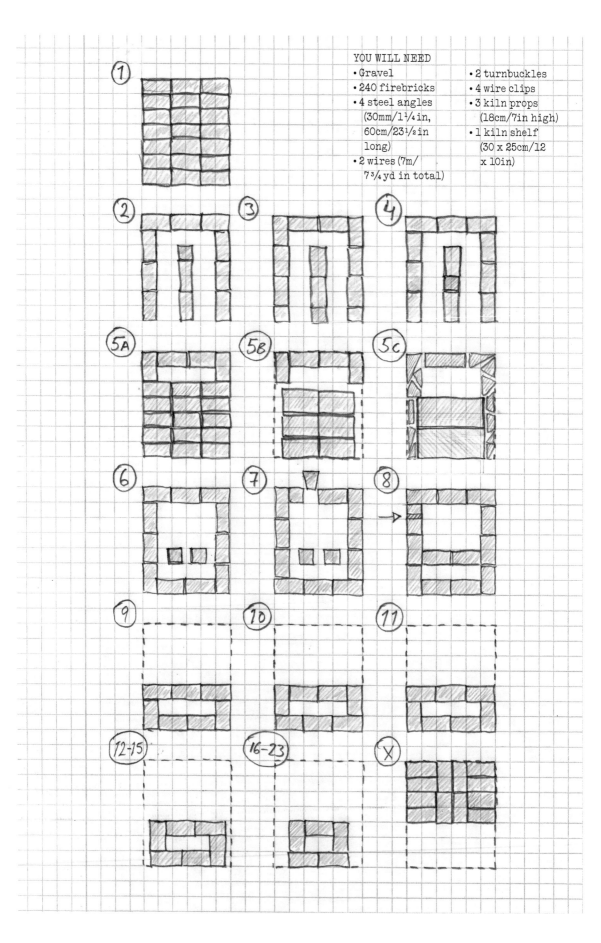

YOU WILL NEED
- Gravel
- 240 firebricks
- 4 steel angles
  (30mm/1¼in,
  60cm/23½in
  long)
- 2 wires (7m/
  7¾yd in total)
- 2 turnbuckles
- 4 wire clips
- 3 kiln props
  (18cm/7in high)
- 1 kiln shelf
  (30 x 25cm/12
  x 10in)

Foundation

Dig down 20cm (8in) at the spot where the kiln will be built. If you are following the brick-by-brick plan an area of 100 x 100cm (40 x 40in) will be enough. Fill the area with gravel. You won't need to lay a concrete slab underneath the kiln, which will save time, money and the environment.

Since the firebox is positioned fairly low down in the kiln, it can be a good idea to raise the whole kiln using one layer of Leca blocks or several layers of cheaper earthenware red bricks in order to get a more comfortable working position during the firing. In the pictures (see pages 122–123) I've raised the kiln using a wooden frame filled with coarse gravel.

1 The base

This should be regarded as the first layer in the kiln and will become the floor for the firebox that protects the foundation from the worst heat. Lay the bricks according to the plan and be extra careful to make it all level from the start to avoid problems higher up.

2–4 The firebox

The firebox is comprised of two channels that meet at the bend going up to the chamber.

5A–5C The floor

The floor extends above the firebox, and the simplest solution is probably to lay the bricks as I have done on the plan. **5A**: It can be a bit of a balancing act to lay them, but once you continue with the build, the bricks on top will keep everything in place. A slightly better alternative is to use a larger brick to cover each channel. **5B**: A relatively standard measurement is 29 x 14.5cm (11½ x 5¾in). If you manage to find a brick that is the same height as the smaller bricks, it can be easier to lay the entire layer using both sizes. The floor can also be made out of one or several kiln shelves that are laid instead of bricks. **5C**: The floor layer doesn't have to have the same height as the other layers. If you build the floor from kiln shelves or larger bricks, you can fill out the rest of the layer using broken pieces of the same material. Any gaps are filled in with clay. The clay will shrink when fired but only a very small amount that won't cause any problems. For a larger permanent kiln, you can also opt to cast a floor using a heat-resistant material.

6–8 The chamber

The chamber is a simple wall laid in a bond. By splitting or sawing a brick you create a gap for the thermocouple (layer 8) and a peephole (layer 7). On a larger kiln you might want two peepholes (one further up and one further down) on the shorter side.

9–23 The chimney

The chimney is built in stages with three narrowing storeys. Three courses the same width as the kiln, four that are half a brick smaller and then a further eight that are smaller still. The last eight courses can be made from earthenware bricks as they won't become so hot that firebricks are necessary. Note that you should lay each course for the chimney in a bond.

Also note that fire will shoot out of the chimney. So it's important to make the chimney high enough to ensure that you don't risk the heat hitting your face if it is very windy, for example. Add to the chimney with several courses to make sure it goes above your head. For each extra course, the kiln will draw more air and fire quicker, but if the chimney gets too high, the kiln will become less efficient.

X The roof

You will take the roof off and put it back on for each firing, and it is through the roof that you load the wares that you want to fire. You actually build the roof as a part of the load and place the last kiln shelf so that it's level with the top course of the chamber. On top of the kiln shelf you place the bricks as insulation.

In the brick-by-brick plan, the chamber is so low that I don't use any layers of shelf for the ware, just three 18-cm (7-in) kiln props with a 30 x 25cm (12 x 10in) kiln shelf at the same height as the top brick layer. Place the props so that they don't weigh down on the parts of the floor that have the least amount of support underneath. It's best to use softbricks for the roof.

If you are only intending to fire raku in the kiln, a great alternative is to place a larger Leca block as a roof without using a kiln shelf and props.

Angles

Finish off by placing steel angles in each corner of the kiln and secure them at the top and bottom using wire and turnbuckles. The angles should be long enough to reach from the base and over the chamber. For the *pytteugn*, the angles are 60cm (23½in) long and 30mm (1¼in) wide.

Tighten the wires enough to hold the bricks in place, but don't tighten them any further as you will then risk damaging the bricks. During firing, the heat will make the bricks expand, and with the resistance from the wire and angles, smaller gaps will get squeezed together.

Extra insulation and surface protection

You can choose to add an extra layer of insulation to the kiln, but it's not necessary for small kilns like this one. It's more important for larger kilns, especially if you have chosen to build it from hardbricks, which don't insulate well and tend to also get hot on the outside. Insulate with a simple clay plaster, which is made by mixing 1 part dry clay with 2 parts sand and 1 part sawdust (all approximate volumes). Add water and mix into a thick paste and coat the outside of the kiln with a 3-cm (1¼-in) thick layer. Apply more as and when any cracks (or other signs of damage) appear. The first time you fire, the plaster will smoke as the sawdust burns.

You can prolong the lifespan of the slightly more fragile softbricks by brushing a thin layer of kiln wash on the inside of the kiln. Since softbricks will absorb moisture, it's good to brush them with clean water before you apply the kiln wash. Don't brush the ceiling with kiln wash since it will easily flake off onto your pots.

Rain and snow protection

Water won't damage the bricks, but it's good if the kiln is protected from rain and snow in between firings. A soaking wet kiln will take longer to get up to temperature, and if you have plastered the kiln with clay you will need to cover the kiln to prevent it from coming off. You can use a tarpaulin or a metal sheet to cover the kiln – you can secure onto the metal angles.

If you want to build a roof over your kiln, I suggest that you make it large enough for the firer (you) and the wood storage to fit underneath it. Cut out a hole in the metal roofing and build the chimney higher so that it reaches 30cm (12in) over the metal sheet. Make sure that no wooden construction gets within 30cm (12in) of the chimney. The chimney can get a draught that is too strong if it ends up significantly higher than the original plan. In that case it's better to raise the foundation of the kiln if that's possible.

Thermocouple and pyrometric cones

It is a lot easier to learn to fire using a thermocouple that shows what temperature the kiln has reached. A thermocouple that measures stoneware temperature is called a Type-S. If you are only firing to earthenware temperature, there are cheaper Type-K thermocouples to buy from various electronic stores.

In addition to the thermocouple, you can use pyrometric cones to measure the temperature. These are small spiky ceramic cones that you place next to the pots in the kiln, clearly visible from the peephole. Each cone melts at one specific temperature. You choose the cones according to whatever cone number your glazes will melt at. When the heat reaches the cone value, the cone will bend and point horizontally instead of pointing upwards.

For your first stoneware firings I suggest that you use an Orton cone 9, which will give you a top temperature of approximately 1280°C (2340°F). Cones don't actually measure temperature, but heatwork. A short period of time at a higher temperature will give the same heatwork as a longer period of time at a slightly lower temperature – this is also how glazes work.

But you don't actually need a thermocouple or firing cones. With a bit of practice, you will be able to see when your glazes are glossy (melted) and how the colour of the flame and the colour inside the kiln changes as the temperature rises.

$\longrightarrow$

A broken brick becomes a perfect little peephole.

126

←
Here I have built up a ledge so that I can position two bricks to partly cover each firebox opening. Doing this controls the combustion and if positioned correctly, you won't need to touch the bricks when adding more wood. Once firing is finished, close the openings completely using another couple of bricks.

→
The roof is built from three kiln props, a kiln shelf and some softbricks. Exactly how you lay the roof is not crucial so you can just use a bit of broken kiln shelf, or one with odd measurements. It's good however if the kiln shelf covers the pots to make sure no particles from the bricks fall on them.

Firing in the kiln

YOU WILL NEED:
- Wood
- Welding gloves
- Pyrometric cones in numbers 9 and 7
- A steel rod, for example 120-cm (47-in) long rebar
- A thermos of coffee

Wadding and other stacking materials for wood-fired kilns

In a wood-fired kiln, the ash from the wood will melt onto the pots and affect the glaze. The longer the firing, the greater the impact.

To prevent the pots from sticking to the kiln furniture it's good to apply kiln wash to the floor and kiln shelves (see recipe on page 48). In the wood-fired kiln I add a thick layer of kiln wash (3–5mm/$\frac{1}{8}$–$\frac{1}{4}$in) that I form into ridges using a serrated throwing rib or scraper. Then I leave the kiln wash to thoroughly dry before loading, which means that the pots will stand on the peaks of the ridged kiln wash. This method will give extra protection against runny glazes and sticky ash, meaning your pots won't stick. Scrape off and apply new kiln wash every 10 firings or so, or when it starts to get glazed over and pots start to stick.

There are many different ways to load a wood-fired kiln using various types of wadding and stacking materials. Often, different methods are combined to give different decorative effects on the finished pots. One of the oldest ways is to stack the pots onto sea shells of different sizes. Shells are basically pure whiting and won't melt during firing. If you want to fire a bowl on shells you take three shells and fill them with clay. Place the shells with the clay facing down and balance the pot on top of the shells. If the shell is thick, you can even glaze the pot underneath and will still be able to get the shells off. After firing, you remove the shells by lowering the pot with the shells into a water bath. The shells will fall off and leave little decorative marks on the glaze and clay.

Personally, I stack a lot of pots onto reed that I harvest in the winters at Alviken (see picture on pages 130–131). What's left after the reed burns is relatively heat resistant. If I have stacked the pots so that they are well protected and the heat is lower

than 1250°C (2280°F), it's usually enough with reed as wadding. The reed will leave burn marks in the form of warm tones and sometimes a small mark on the clay will appear where the reed hasn't really been sufficient as wadding, but those can be fun effects.

Directing the flame in the kiln

The way the brick-by-brick plan on page 124 is designed means that it's almost impossible to load it incorrectly, but if the kiln ends up slightly larger it can be relevant to consider how the flame will move through it. The areas that the flame doesn't reach will be more difficult to get up to a high temperature. To help you direct the flame you have the kiln furniture as well as the pots, which will physically push and steer the fire on its way through the kiln.

In this type of kiln, the flame will steer towards the middle and top of the kiln, and to get an even temperature you need to attempt to direct the heat to the lower part of the kiln. If you have one or more kiln shelves you can guide the flame downwards in, the kiln by dividing the opening into the chimney between the kiln shelves. A good rule of thumb is to place the first kiln shelf high enough to get two-thirds of the opening underneath it. If you then push the shelf up against the opening, the flame will have to go underneath the shelf to reach the chimney.

After firing, check where the colder areas were and think about why the flame didn't reach them. Can you position a pot so that it nudges the flame in that direction a bit more next time, or is it an area that is better suited for something that needs firing to a lower temperature?

Wood

For the *pytteugn* you will need thinly split wood, preferably around 50cm (20in) long. If the pieces of wood are too short, it will become more difficult to feed in and if they are too thick, it won't burn well in the small space. The optimum size of wood has a thickness of 3–5cm (1$\frac{1}{4}$–2in).

All types of wood will work well, and if you can get hold of old timber from the wood industry this will usually work perfectly well. If you have a choice, I would suggest that you use softwood for your first

firings. Softwood will give a lot of flame and will burn away easily in the firebox.

It's important that the wood is dry. Wood that is nice and dry will give off a ringing sound when you hit two pieces against each other and will burn without leaving a lot of embers. Freshly chopped wood that is left to dry will as a rule need 6–12 months to become dry enough for a wood-fired kiln.

For your first firing I suggest that you have 1 cubic metre (35 cubic feet) of wood, cut to size and stacked next to the kiln so that you can concentrate on firing.

Lighting the wood-fired kiln (0–800°C/1470°F)
Light the kiln using small pieces of kindling in one of the two fireboxes. Keep the other firebox closed with a couple of bricks, while the one that you have started the fire in can be wide open at this stage.

If you have wares that haven't been bisque-fired you will need to fire very carefully and follow the firing schedule for single firing on page 48. If the flames get into the chamber too early the pots will get damaged, and when a kiln is as small as a *pytteugn* it can be easier to mainly fire bisque-fired wares. For bisque-fired wares you can as a rule take 2 hours to reach 600°C (1110°F), which is a lot quicker than a standard glaze firing. Light the second firebox (channel) when you have reached 600°C (1110°F).

At this stage of the firing, the kiln will work as a standard bonfire – if you add wood, the temperature will rise. The temperature will generally rise very easily, so fire slowly and methodically and try to avoid getting anything more than thin smoke from the chimney, ideally none at all.

Body reduction (850–1150°C/1560–2100°F)
At this stage you will have fires going in both fireboxes and you will be able to see that the pots have started to glow. At 850°C (1560°F) the pots will glow a red colour

←
The pressed plates from pages
80–90 are ready for firing. I use
reed from the lake near where I
live as wadding.

that at 1000°C (1800°F) slowly turns orange, finally turning yellow and white before firing is complete. The first time it can be difficult to see, but look at the insides of the pots to see if they are glowing or not.

In order for the heat to rise well at this stage you'll want to cover half of each opening on both fireboxes with a brick. This way you prevent cold air flowing through the firebox. Add more wood so that smoke comes out of the chimney. Each time you add wood, it's good to push back one of the already burning pieces of wood at the front of the firebox to the back. Try to get the wood into the areas with the least amount of wood.

Seal any visible cracks around the kiln by brushing on a mixture of clay and sand. Mix one part sand with one part clay and add water until you have a consistency of thin yogurt. The ratios are approximate, so add more clay or sand if it gets too wet.

At this stage of firing, the kiln will start to change its behaviour and you will need to find a balance between feeding the fire and waiting. It can be easier to control if you alternate between the two fireboxes when adding wood. If the fire flows through the pots, the temperature is probably rising, and once you reach around 1000°C (1800°F) the fire will protrude out of the chimney. Add more wood when the fire retracts from the chimney and you will be able to maintain a continuous rise in temperature. If you add wood too early or add too much, heavy smoke will come out of the chimney and the kiln's temperature will drop. This is because a heavy reduction will actually cool down the kiln – if this happens, wait until the smoke eases and take it slower when adding the wood.

The smoke from the chimney at this stage means not only that the kiln's temperature is rising but also that the clay is being reduced, which makes clays containing iron turn a red-brown colour and porcelain turn a cold, white colour. The reduced clay will also affect the glaze that coats it and many colours and effects can appear. On the side that is facing the fire, a steel grey tone can appear if you keep a steady and heavy reduction.

Top temperature (1150–1280°C/2100–2340°F)
For the final temperature increase you will need to create two very hot fireboxes. Continue to feed the fire,

alternating between the two holes. You will notice that the kiln will need feeding more often. Aim to get half of the height of the firebox filled with embers and the space above filled with fire. When the combustion is working well, you can hear the draught through the firebox, and when it quietens you are probably letting in cold air that will cool the fireboxes. You will also be able to see that the fire isn't filling out the firebox in the same way. In practice, this means that you should add more wood before the fire has retracted from the top of the chimney. It can help to close the opening to the firebox by 5cm (2in) more to control the air inside the kiln – test it out to see if it helps.

Don't panic if the temperature doesn't rise, fire methodically and the kiln's temperature will rise as long as the fire reaches the chamber. What can happen is that the layer of embers grows and prevents the fire from flowing freely through the kiln. Stir the burning wood with an iron rod or a piece of wood if this happens. You don't need to rake out the hot embers, often it's enough to stir them a little to burn them up.

Finishing

When you see that your cone has started to bend, firing is complete. The first time you fire in the *pytteugn* you should allow 4 hours from start to finish, but with some practice it can be done a lot quicker. It's a good idea to hold the temperature steady for 10 minutes at the end to soak the kiln and then finish off by completely shutting the openings to the fireboxes. You can also place a kiln shelf on top of the chimney to calm down the cooling. It's not unusual for the *pytteugn* to be cool enough to open after 4 hours.

Different methods of firing

You can make many variations to the firing schedule to get different results on your finished wares, and a small kiln is great for experimenting.

If you want more effects from the wood, I suggest that you do a longer firing. I have let kilns like this keep the top temperature for 12 hours in order to get melted ash deposits on the pots.

Another alternative is to vary the cooling. If you finish off the kiln as I describe above, you get an oxidation cooling, where oxygen flows freely around the pots, giving strong colours and glossy glazes. The same glazes and clays develop a more muted colour range and matt surfaces in a reduction cooling. You achieve a reduction cooling by filling the fireboxes completely with wood as the last thing you do before closing the kiln (fireboxes and chimney). When you do this, smoke and fire will seep out through all cracks in the kiln and the temperature will reduce quickly.

$\longrightarrow$

Bending cone next to upside-down bowls.

TROUBLESHOOTING
- If your pots get blisters during firing, the reduction has happened too early, that is, the kiln has smoked too early. If you know that smoke came out of the kiln before 850°C (1560°F) the solution might be to avoid this in the next firing. Some clays (often dark ones) are especially prone to this, since they contain a lot of organic material that in itself creates smoke. You can bisque fire these clays longer to burn off the extra organic material.

- If the layer of embers is too high despite you stirring it regularly, it's probably to do with the wood. Try to use finer splinted wood. This tends to happen if the wood is damp or if you feed the kiln too often or too much.
- If you have difficulties getting the temperature to rise the last 50°C (120°F), it is generally because the fireboxes aren't getting hot enough. Do you have a brick covering half of each opening so you're not letting in too much cold air? Are you

adding enough wood to fill the fireboxes with fire, and can the fire flow freely through the kiln? Test systematically and see if small changes can get the temperature to rise. If the wood is damp or rotten it will be difficult, if not impossible, for the temperature to rise.
- If the glazes crawl or flake during firing, it can be due to the kiln and pots being too damp. Take it slower up to 200°C (390°F) to dry out both the pots and the kiln before you let the heat increase.

Firing in a larger kiln

Pages 140–143: When sketching out new vases, plates and bowls, I'm already planning where in the kiln they should go depending on what decorative effect I'm after.

To fill the kiln, I need to work for about a month in the workshop. The loading is done efficiently over a couple of days — both in the summer and in the winter. My wife's large sculptures are usually at the back, since they benefit from the slightly lower temperature and the slower increase of heat in that spot.

145

My large wood-fired kiln is just
under 6 metres (20 feet) long and
is built from 15 tons (16½ US tons)
firebricks and 45 tons (50 US tons)
gravel. At the time of writing, the
kiln has been in use for 5 years
and the walls have become ragged,
shiny and colourful from fire and
ash. I have begun to get to know
her fairly well and believe she
will last for many years to come.
I know which direction the fire
wants to take, when she wants
a lot of wood and which effects
I can expect from firing in
different ways.

We take it in turns feeding the kiln — me, my wife Matilda, mum and dad — and have done so ever since the first firing. It takes technique and experience to be able to control the kiln to get a good result, and concentration is crucial so that we can read the kiln's signals. Throughout almost the whole firing process we have to add more wood every 5 minutes or so. The time in between we use to fetch more wood and to evaluate the process via exterior signals such as smoke, fire and shifts in temperature. Most challenging is working in hot weather with temperatures of over 1300°C (2370°F) inside the kiln, but in a way, I enjoy the experience of getting tired out and following the rhythm of the kiln more and more closely.

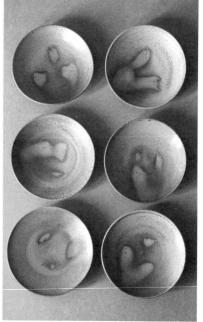

Index

155

First published in the United Kingdom in 2021 by
Pavilion
An imprint of HarperCollins*Publishers*
1 London Bridge Street
London SE1 9GF

www.harpercollins.co.uk

HarperCollins*Publishers*
Macken House
39/40 Mayor Street Upper
Dublin 1
D01 C9W8
Ireland

ISBN 978-1-911663-287

A CIP catalogue record for this book is available
from the British Library.

10 9 8 7 6 5 4 3 2

Reproduction by Rival Colour Ltd
Printed in Malaysia

www.pavilionbooks.com

Publisher: Helen Lewis
Editor: Izzy Holton
Designer: Alice Kennedy-Owen
Production Controller: Phil Brown

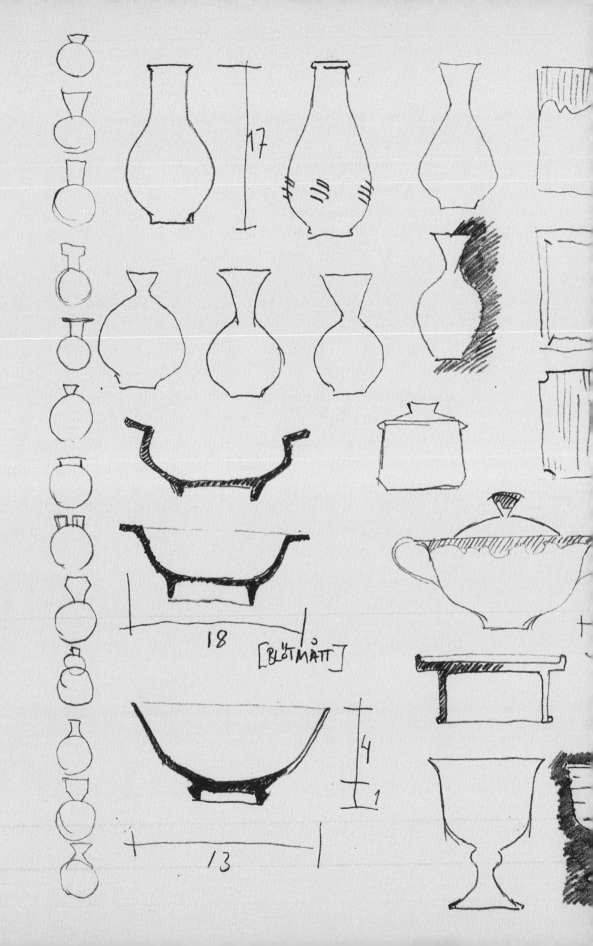

17

18

[BLÖTMATT]

1/4

1

13